What people are  saying about

The Language of Flowers
in the Time of COVID

When the onset of the pandemic upends cherished plans for a flower temple pilgrimage in Japan, Stamm combines her knowledge of flower symbolism and Buddhist teachings to navigate a year of global loss, anxiety, disappointment, despair, and unrest — all through the wisdom of flowers. Deeply informed and insightful, this book relates the spiritual pilgrimage nearly all of us took courtesy of COVID, a journey into a great and fearsome unknown.
Karen Maezen Miller, author of *Paradise in Plain Sight: Lessons from a Zen Garden*

This book, spirited, intimate, and thoughtful, stands with the pulse of suffering humanity in a tangle of crises while held in a landscape of extraordinary beauty and resilience. The writing blossoms Buddha Mind. We are struck through with nature's transcendent presence in the complexity of the song of a flower, healing the heart in a time of global anguish. A very special treasure.
Eido Frances Carney Roshi, Teacher & Abbess, Olympia Zen Center; author of *Kakurenbo or the Whereabouts of Zen Priest Ryokan*

A tale of the healing power of flowers: Stamm meets 2020's unbelievable shifts and changes as a journey of transformation. We travel together with Joan from deep disappointment and shock through a gradual dawning of acceptance of the ancient truths of impermanence. The seasons of that difficult year unfold as flowers bud, bloom, and fade. Plans are made, perfected, and abandoned. Along the way we're joined by Zen and ikebana masters, heroic Chinese doctors, wise and corrupt American politicians, and passionate protestors as we return again and again to a quiet garden on a mountain on an island. A reflection sad, hopeful and wise.

Nomon Tim Burnett, Guiding Teacher, Red Cedar Zen Community; and Executive Director of Mindfulness Northwest

Joan has skillfully interwoven our collective experience during the pandemic with the enlightened teachings from the flower world. We can always look to flowers, and this book, to remind us of the preciousness of our existence, and that even in unprecedented times, we live within the cycles of nature. Flowers can be our teachers to guide us through all of the seasons of our lives.

Anjie Cho, dharma arts teacher at Shambhala Center New York; and author of *Holistic Spaces: 108 Ways to Create a Mindful and Peaceful Home*

The Language of Flowers in the Time of COVID

Finding Solace in Zen, Nature and Ikebana

The Language of Flowers in the Time of COVID

Finding Solace in Zen, Nature and Ikebana

Joan D. Stamm

MANTRA
BOOKS

Winchester, UK
Washington, USA

JOHN HUNT PUBLISHING

First published by Mantra Books, 2023
Mantra Books is an imprint of John Hunt Publishing Ltd., No. 3 East Street, Alresford
Hampshire SO24 9EE, UK
office@jhpbooks.com
www.johnhuntpublishing.com
www.mantra-books.net

For distributor details and how to order please visit the 'Ordering' section on our website.

ISBN: 978 1 80341 190 3
978 1 80341 191 0 (ebook)
Library of Congress Control Number: 2022909435

A CIP catalogue record for this book is available from the British Library.

Design: Matthew Greenfield

UK: Printed and bound by CPI Group (UK) Ltd, Croydon, CR0 4YY
Printed in North America by CPI GPS partners

We operate a distinctive and ethical publishing philosophy in
all areas of our business, from our global network of authors to
production and worldwide distribution.

Contents

In memory of all those who succumbed to COVID-19

Previous Books
A Pilgrimage in Japan:
the 33 Temples of Kannon
ISBN: 978 1 78535 750 3

Heaven and Earth are Flowers:
Reflections on Ikebana and Buddhism
ISBN: 0 86171 577 2

Permissions and Credits

The haiku "blooming flowers…," "in the field…," and "by itself…," by Issa were translated by David G. Lanoue in *Pure Land Haiku: The Art of Priest Issa,* and appear with his permission.

The haiku "a petal shower…" by Basho, "the camellia…" by Buson, "what a strange thing…" and "flowers scattering…" by Issa appear in *The Essential Haiku: Versions of Basho, Buson and Issa* by Robert Hass.

The haiku "all beings are flowers…" by Soen Nakagawa, appear in *Endless Vow: The Zen Path of Soen Nakagawa* by Kazuaki Tanahashi and Roko Sherry Chayat.

The haiku "the spirit, the truth…" by Kikusha-ni, and "a white lotus…" by Buson, appear in *Haiku Mind: 108 Poems to Cultivate Awareness and Open Your Heart* by Patricia Donegan.

The haiku "white chrysanthemum…," "full moon…," and "purple cloud…" by Chiyo-ni appear in *Chiyo-ni: Woman Haiku Master* by Patricia Donegan and Yoshie Ishibashi.

The haiku "we human beings…" by Issa, and "about to bloom…" by Buson, appear in *Haiku: Vol.2 & 3* by R.H. Blyth.

The haiku "exhausted…" by Basho appears in *A Zen Wave: Bash's Haiku and Zen* by Robert Aitken.

Acknowledgements

A deep bow goes to:

My sister Gwen and main companion during the endless pandemic days of seclusion and lockdowns. Her friendship made the long months of isolation bearable;

All the essential workers: health care personnel, grocery clerks, waiters and waitresses, ferry workers, retail clerks, and so many others who risked their lives and kept it all going during the pandemic;

My editor and publisher for bringing this book into print;

Bruce Hamana for his beautiful lotus photograph;

The many plants and flowers that give of themselves throughout the seasons, through heat and cold, drought and snow, without even one whimper of complaint. Thank you for the solace you freely offer;

The ceramic artists and basket weavers who create beautiful vessels used in ikebana, especially Mika McCann, Paddy McNeely, Reid Ozaki, and many others whose names are unknown to me;

Those who took the time to read my manuscript and offer their reviews;

The many Buddhist teachers and teachings that provided wisdom and the voice of sanity during the darkest times of 2020 and beyond, especially my teacher Eido Frances Carney Roshi at the Olympia Zen Center; and

All those who I've forgotten or neglected to mention, but who contributed in some way to the culmination of this book.

A heartfelt thank you to all.

Chrysanthemum, cordyline leaves, pine, huckleberry

Preface

full moon —
keeping it in my eyes
on a distant walk
Chiyo-ni

The "Great Mystery," that unnamed, and many named, universal force that operates in its own way, in its own time, in unique and complex patterns too intricate to comprehend by the human brain, had laid out a plan for 2020 that nobody, except for a few infectious disease experts, saw coming. A "never seen before" virus—spherical with little viral spikes or knobs—resulted in pneumonia with deadly consequences. Before anyone knew what was happening, we would all be kowtowing to this microscopic menace because none of us wanted to look death in the face, just yet.

My plan for 2020, one among millions throughout the world, did *not* involve kowtowing to anything. Nor did it involve, "Staying Home." *My* plan, hatched months—even years—earlier with great care and hours of research, involved spending the month of April in Japan exploring a flower temple pilgrimage in the Kansai region—all part of an investigation into the deeper meaning of *hanakotoba*: the language of flowers.

The virus didn't care.

First detected in China, this novel coronavirus would rapidly consume the world. How we, as mere humans and world citizens—budding bodhisattvas—would grapple with its spread and consequences, with all that it unveiled and revealed in our culture, would be the story of 2020. All the while, another phenomenon, not of human making, and more ancient than the beginning of humans on earth, would quietly and with great dignity play out in the background. Mother Earth, the way she tilted toward or away from the sun, spun the narrative of

1

nature: the changing seasons and weather patterns, the budding and blooming of flowers, the withering and falling of leaves, and the mystery of winter's long sleep.

As an ikebana practitioner and teacher, Zen Buddhist and former expat, Japanese culture had inspired my creative bent ever since 1991 when I taught English in Kobe. Back then I fantasized about becoming fluent in the language, finding a Japanese boyfriend, studying Zen, and staying forever. But the year I arrived, Japan's economy crashed. A ten-year period called "the Lost Decade" ensued. By 1992, my hopes and dreams, my livelihood, and Japan-dream-fantasy-world sunk under the shadows of an economic downturn. By 1993, with hours cut, jobs scarce, and friends moving back home, I too began to contemplate returning to the US. The Japanese boyfriend never materialized; my opportunity to study Zen with a local monk fizzled out; my passion for ikebana had not yet emerged. Isolation and dwindling employment prospects compelled me to reluctantly pack up the two suitcases I'd arrived with and book a flight home. The month was August, and as anyone knows who's spent a summer in Japan, luck would have me leaving *that* for the coolness of the Pacific Northwest. Even so, reverse culture shock and an uncanny homesickness for the country I left behind soon stirred a longing to return—after all, August in Japan also means lotus blossoms. The layered nuances of ancient art forms and Buddhist thought, the haunting beauty of centuries-old temples, serene gardens and vermillion pagodas tugged at my heartstrings. Ever since those days of being introduced to a culture radically different than my own, I've been unraveling threads of inspiration, all of them connected to Japanese art forms and Buddhist philosophy—*always keeping an eye on the full moon.*

With a background in art, and a love of flowers, my creative "thread" led to ikebana; my spiritual "thread" to Zen. Throughout the years, I would find a variety of reasons to

2

travel back to Japan. This habit continued to be nurtured with ikebana lessons at Daikakuji Temple, my school's headquarters; with a Buddhist pilgrimage to the 33 temples of Kannon; and the discovery of a Jodo Shinshu Reiki master from Kyoto. The exploration of my latest "obsession": "The Twenty-five Flower Temples of the Kansai" — meant to commence April 1, 2020 — fed my passion for ikebana, Buddhism and the hidden language of flowers, a dynamic threesome that held potential worth exploring. On April Fool's Day, I planned to be on a non-stop flight to Osaka with friend Kandis and her brother Robert to research first-hand a smattering of "flower temples": ancient Buddhist sites that had been expanding and transforming their grounds into gardens for decades. A glossy Japanese magazine: *KIE*, or *Kateigaho International Edition*, Spring/Summer issue, 2010, featured an article titled, "50 Temples and Their Flowers: A Pilgrimage." I had marked the page years ago, and tucked the idea into a brain file called "Possibilities." Someday, I thought, I'll visit those flower temples.

In 2019, resurrecting a creative spark buried under three years of gloomy moods and creative drought, "Someday" arrived. I dusted off my *KIE*, found an address and sent an old-fashioned letter in a blue airmail envelope to the abbot who'd hatched the idea of a flower temple pilgrimage. Some time later, after I'd nearly forgotten my letter, an email with kanji characters in the subject line appeared in my inbox. A friend of the founding abbot, a Reverend Yuya Tomamatsu at Temple #7, had been enlisted to respond. Ah, a validation from the universe perhaps?

Before long, plans solidified to have us arriving in Japan the following year in time for the iconic cherry blossoms: the universal poetic representatives of impermanence. *Hanami* would launch this tale into a journey of flower symbolism and flower "language," interpreted through the lens of Buddhism. I would research and write about flowers, the spiritual nature of flowers, flower temple pilgrimages and the changing face of Japanese Buddhism.

Flowers and trees, and the spirits of flowers and trees, figure prominently in many Japanese art forms. In Noh plays in particular, the spirit of a plant or flower often appear in human form, usually to a traveling monk, who represents the author's intent to tell a Buddhist story. In the play *Basho,* for example, a middle-aged woman appears to the typical unsuspecting monk, but she is in reality the spirit of the *basho,* or banana tree. In an article by Dr. Paul Atkins, titled, "The Enlightenment of Plants and Trees in Noh Drama" he proposes that, "The choice of the basho is especially apt; its long, ribbed leaves look wonderful in summer, but are shredded by autumn and winter winds, reminding us of the impermanence of life."

Nature gives us endless metaphors for impermanence, but in 2020 our impermanence contemplation, our "shredded leaves," did not show up as the basho tree, or the representative cherry blossoms that bud, bloom and scatter in two weeks. The face of impermanence would manifest as a virus, one never seen before, one that would officially be named SARS-CoV-2: severe acute respiratory syndrome coronavirus 2, or novel coronavirus. The virus would change our view of reality overnight, demonstrate again and again our inter-connection with all beings, and the unreliability of everything we thought was reliable; it would challenge us to choose human life over livelihood, national debt over rampant homelessness, truth over lies.

"The trunk of the basho tree," Dr. Atkins said, "is merely a layer of leaves; remove them and the center is hollow, just as the material world only appears to have substance, according to the Buddhist worldview." In the Noh play "the only beings attaining enlightenment are the priest and the audience; the basho plant was already enlightened."

In Noh drama, a uniquely Japanese theatrical form that incorporates Buddhist ideas into haunting storylines, the suggestion that plants and flowers are already enlightened presented an intriguing notion. Perhaps flowers in their pure presentation represented a state of nirvana, of being beyond the realm of human suffering; or perhaps by contemplating their nature they led us to that place. Through a series of reflections on the heart or essence of flowers: plum, cherry, daffodil, kerria, wisteria, peony... within the hallowed confines of ancient Japanese Buddhist temple gardens, I had hoped to come closer to the heart of this matter. But then the virus came along, changing everyone's life plans and reorienting us in various ways.

In our new world of the novel coronavirus and universal "stay home" directives, reflections soon turned toward the confines of my forested home: six and a half acres on a mountain, on an island, in the Salish Sea. Shantideva the eighth-century Buddhist monk, and author of *Guide to the Bodhisattva's Way of Life*, had brought me to this mountain many years ago. Alone at a silent retreat in the wilds of Scotland in the days when I sought liberation in the "wilds," and one month before September 11, 2001, I came across these lines and something stirred:

When shall I withdraw into the forest,
And live among the trees,
With birds and deer who say nothing unpleasant
But are a joy to live with?

A city dweller for over 25 years, I yearned to live in the country closer to nature. It would take another 7 years to free myself from urban life, and find a "forest" where "birds and deer say nothing unpleasant," a place of quiet solitude four hours from any major city.

Growing flowers for ikebana, flowers for every season, had been one of my goals; but growing flowers one might encounter in Japan—a secondary goal—proved to be more difficult in my new mountain habitat. Poor soil, mossy boulders, and hungry deer led to numerous failures; but the successes, along with native plants that inspired many Natural Scene arrangements, fed my ikebana mind. In 2020, with a deadly virus overtaking the world, and deprived of my Japanese adventure, I soon turned to my own plot of paradise—the 1300-foot level of my mountain garden—to explore the interwoven worlds of nature and human nature. Supplemented by lowland places, friends' gardens, public squares, parks, cemeteries, and the virtual gardens that came through YouTube and weblinks, I began to contemplate the language of flowers within the context of a pandemic. While we humans grappled with an invisible enemy, the seasons continued undaunted. Flowers, destined to bud, bloom and scatter, unfolded as symbolic backdrops to changing world events, to the pernicious virus that hunted us. COVID-19, soon to be the new name issued by the World Health Organization, would give us great pause in the Japanese calendar year of "beautiful harmony" or *Reiwa* 2—known in the Gregorian calendar as 2020, a year some called a time of "clear seeing" or "perfect vision." What would the virus help us see? I couldn't tell in the beginning, but I hoped something significant would emerge for everyone to see, something that would move the world forward into a more compassionate and cooperative place. But hope being what it is—a dreamworld of wishful thinking, or, as Joko Beck points out in *Everyday Zen*, a mind that takes us out of the present moment—I'd have to wait and see. No guarantees. By grounding myself in Zen teachings, and keeping my eye on that "full moon," I vowed to practice suspending "hope" in favor of being with "the way it is." Not an easy vow to keep. Determined to make the most of my isolation, and hunkered down with books, writing, creative projects and a routine walking and meditation practice, I vowed to be content.

But before that time of social distancing and my hermit-like life, in the first two months of 2020, when Kandis, Robert and I still planned to spend the month of April in Japan, the dawning of our new world had not yet arrived. In the Time of Plum (February), the beginning of spring in the ancient Japanese almanac, world events quietly but rapidly began to transform.

Chapter 1

Plum in the Time of COVID

in the field
of the Buddha of Misfortune
plum blossoms!
Issa

The arrival of plum blossoms—a time of hope and endurance? Or, as some believed in ancient times, a protection against evil?

In the Buddhist view, events, phenomena, the workings of individual and collective life—cause and effect, or karma—comprise a complex web of interconnection so vast and profound as to be beyond human comprehension. Yet in the time of plum, compelled to unravel the relative events of the world, to pinpoint beginnings and junctures—at least the appearance of such things—the question, "How *did* this new reality begin?" deserved an answer. When did the virus sail across the Pacific Ocean to the shores of my home state of Washington? How would it, or could it, possibly cross paths with the ideas and inspirations of the "Flower Temples" of Japan?

According to the Heart Sutra, an ancient Buddhist teaching on impermanence and inter-connection, there is no beginning or end, no birth or death. All things in essence are interdependent—a piece of paper, explains Thich Nhat Hanh, reflects sun, rain, trees, loggers... an endless stream of causes and conditions, one moving seamlessly into the other without our noticing. We think phenomena are independent because that is how they appear. But human lives do not exist alone and disconnected, we do not live and die in the sense of existing or not existing, but transform into something else, and something else....

Cause and effect... you remember an article in a glossy

Japanese magazine from ten years ago and the next thing you know you're inviting a friend on a trip to Japan. "Yes, I'd love to spend April in Kyoto," she says, and you start booking rooms, flights, shuttles.... Then the Ancient Japanese Almanac announces: "Spring Winds Thaw the Ice"; it is February, 2020, a time when life as we knew it began to come undone—another beginning, another ending. The first plums begin to show buds. The first person contracts a strange new disease. Plum blossoms open. The first person dies of this strange new disease. All beginnings, all endings, all neither and both—one event flowing into another and another....

Did the virus come from a bat? A pangolin? A lab? Theories, suspicions, speculations and paranoia circulated freely.

Consider this one: an animal poacher in Hubei Province, a man who sold pangolins and other exotic animals in the black market of Wuhan, brought the virus in from the wilds: places where humans should tread with caution. The pangolin, an unassuming slow-moving mammal with a smooth round snout and innocent eyes may have innocently played host to a virus carried by a bat, a bat from a cave, or a bat in another cage above or near the pangolin's.

After the supposed bat, defecated or urinated or bled onto the supposed pangolin, or directly onto a human, inadvertently transferring a "novel" or, "never seen before in our life time," virus, it took off like..., dare I say it, a bat out of hell. People in Wuhan started getting sick, really sick, with body aches, fever, dry cough, and difficulty breathing. Some of them ended up in the ICU. Some of them died. A Dr. Li Wenliang noticed something different about the type of pneumonia he was seeing and posted warnings to friends on social media. The authorities accused him of "rumor-mongering." More people got sick. More people died.

Pangolins *are* bought, sold, and traded by the thousands, that's not a theory. A rare and critically endangered anteater that looks like a cross between an armadillo and an opossum, pangolins are the most trafficked mammal in the world. They are illegally traded, not only for their "tasty" meat but supposed medicinal scales. A pangolin currently sells on the underground market for $300 a pound.

Even though an endangered species, in 2019 nine tons of pangolin scales along with one thousand elephant tusks were seized in Hong Kong enroute from Nigeria to Vietnam. Later that year, and back in my little world on the mountain, around the time pangolins were being slaughtered for the upcoming Lunar New Year, *Pimsleur's Japanese I* re-taught me how to say phrases I'd learned, forgotten and relearned half a dozen times: how to ask for and understand directions; how to order food for others; how to get on the right train; how to say, *Motto yukkuri onegaishimasu*, "Speak more slowly, please."

When I wasn't studying Japanese phrases, I fine-tuned a four-page itinerary on a twenty-five-day "flower temple" spring-fest whirlwind that would encompass Kyoto, Nara, Kanazawa, Mt. Yoshino and Koyasan.

All the while, said hunter/farmer caught his bats, pangolins, civets or something else, took them along with his chickens, pigs and ducks to a "wet market" where cages of live animals, stacked one on top of the other, awaited slaughter. A virus not lethal to the pangolin, or the bat, theoretically transferred from host to human via bodily parts or fluids: intestines, blood, urine, feces; which ran like rivers through the markets of Wuhan (not so different from our own factory farms where animals await the stun gun packed neck to neck, and beak to beak, wallowing in pens and cages smeared with their own excrement).

But the story of the pangolin and the bat and the live animal market in Wuhan is all conjecture. Nobody knows with any certainty where the novel coronavirus that results in a deadly pneumonia originated. Based on data regarding SARS: linked to palm civet cats; MERS: a bat virus that jumped to camels then humans; Ebola: a bat virus that jumped to apes then humans; and AIDS: linked to chimpanzees; this new virus appeared, at least preliminarily, to have originated in a horseshoe bat and may have jumped to a pangolin or some other animal and then to a human somewhere in China. In February, 2020, that's all anyone knew for sure.

Despite dismal accounts coming out of the People's Republic, we were still in the season of plum—betting on hope and endurance, with a touch of excitement, a bit of joy, a bit of *yama warau*, a Japanese phrase that means "the mountains are joyful" with spring. Plum is about to bloom. Winter was waning, although not officially over, and plentiful spring buds and blooms were on their way. Even under snow, the plum continues to bloom, earning it the reputation of "strength in the midst of adversity," which is why poets favor it over cherry; and why, in Japan, it is one of the "three friends of winter." Together with bamboo and pine, a trilogy of endurance, flexibility and longevity can be expressed. Bamboo, plum and pine also symbolized Buddha, Confucius, and Lao Tzu (respectively), another threesome that brought wisdom, order and personal freedom into the world. In Japan these three patriarchs would find a happy home, and establish a unique culture and society.

In January of 2020, we didn't know it yet, but we would need endurance and flexibility; we would contemplate longevity and mortality in new ways; we would re-examine the meaning of "evil," and hope for wisdom and order. As for joy? It would come as a gift from nature, from flowers that bloomed for no one in particular and dispelled the opposite of joy. But before the dark days arrived, I and most other Americans were preoccupied with our "normal" lives—in my case with planning the Japan trip, preparing for two ikebana events in Seattle, and teaching ikebana classes. The focus of my first class in February would be the "three friends of winter" triad. Not having any plum or bamboo on the mountain, I put the word out. Together with shore pine, which grew abundantly on the mountain, we would finally, after our snow-day cancellation, get around to creating a "three friends" *seika* in the heaven, earth, human configuration.

On the island, word travels fast. One of my students, together with a friend's professional pruner, found enough plum branches for my two classes. Kandis offered beautiful bamboo from a grove that ran freely down by her pond. With my shore pine and mugos, the three friends materialized.

Before that first February class, SARS-Cov-2 had already jumped across the Sea of Japan into the Land of the Rising Sun, and into the US too, although we didn't know it yet; Japan issued travel advisories, but mostly for people from China and Thailand. From the vantage point of months later, this event should have sounded the pandemic alarm, but at the time, believe it or not—and it is frankly hard to believe—it didn't. The average person on the street didn't think this strange new virus discovered in China posed much of a threat to North America. Like millions of others, I initially thought the media exploited the drama. Wasn't this just another virus like the flu? *Nothing to worry about,* the White House kept telling us. The president, the Center for Disease Control, the World Health Organization— did any of them sound the alarm? Didn't the president keep saying that thousands of people die of the flu every year? That was our state of denial or delusion or complacency back then. Not until the Time of Cosmos would we learn through Bob Woodward's presidential interviews for his forthcoming book, *Rage,* that the top leader of our country knew that this virus was "deadly stuff... more deadly than the flu." Rather than institute immediate federal emergency action to mitigate spread, the president pretended that the virus was nothing for the public to worry about—and some still insinuated that the virus was a Democratic hoax.

Between my first ikebana class in February and my second one two weeks later, something big started happening aboard a cruise ship called the Diamond Princess, a 13-decker ship carrying 3700 crew and passengers. On its way back from Okinawa after a 14-day cruise around China, Vietnam, and Taiwan, the ship was suddenly told to return to Tokyo Bay. Authorities kept everyone on board until health care workers tested passengers and crew. The strange new virus, first detected in China, had somehow gotten aboard the ship undetected. Time dragged on. People got sick. More people got sick; all together 700 passengers got sick and 14 would die. Later the Diamond Princess would serve as an example of "symptomless spreading," the pernicious quality of this virus, a stealthy stalker that could infect and transmit secretly. A text message from Kandis, "How are you feeling about traveling with this virus?"

Initially, the answer was, "Not too worried." The cruise ship in Yokohama, although dire and tragic, remained a long way away from Kyoto. I thought it was a one-time, rare and isolated event.

Still, I emailed the manager of our inn to inquire about cases in Kyoto. His internet search uncovered 2 cases (this was in a city of 1.5 million). He advised us to take precautions. Bring hand sanitizer and face masks. *Face masks?* (Common in Japan any time of year, Japanese wore surgical masks to prevent the spread of colds. Foreigners did not. We thought the custom was…, well, a little weird.) I relayed the inn manager's suggestions to my friends and for the moment they seemed calmed. The trip was still on.

Later I would note that the day before my first spring class, February 7, Dr. Li Wenliang, the 33-year-old Chinese ophthalmologist who worked in Wuhan Central Hospital, the brave unsuspecting soul who tried to warn others of the dangers of this new coronavirus, had died. His parents contracted the disease too. They survived. Later Dr. Li would be hailed a "martyr": in China someone who gave his life for his country.

He left behind a pregnant wife and young son.

Dr. Li's death, and those of several other doctors in China, should have been yet another alarm. This was not a disease that only took the aged and infirm, but the young, the healthy. Four days after Dr. Li's death, the disease that killed him was officially named COVID-19 (coronavirus disease 2019) to avoid the stigma that could arise if a place, people or animal were named. The president would later coin the terms "China flu" and "kung flu."

My life in America continued normally: a trip to see my Zen teacher and partake in a belated New Year's poetry reading; a routine visit to dentist and doctor; shopping; dining out; drinking matcha lattes at the local coffee shop—all per usual. I planned for my next ikebana class.

On a trip to town to pick up mail, I noticed piles of budded branches in my neighbor's yard. Every spring I admired the five mature plum trees that bloomed in cotton candy pink in front of their pale aqua double-wide. On my way back I stopped to inquire. The curtains were drawn, but smoke billowed out the chimney. An older gentleman wearing a knit cardigan opened the front door.

When I explained that I lived up the road at the top of the hill, that I taught Japanese flower-arranging, he said, "Oh take as many as you want. I guess the guys are gonna chip 'em."

Oh, the chipper, sin of sins. To think of all those budded branches disappearing into the hungry mouth of a chipper... well, they literally screamed to be rescued.

I gathered as many as would fit in the back of my car, and readied them for class in buckets of water. What a find! I had enough for my students and for me, with plenty of extras for the days ahead. In my excitement I didn't notice the latest headline, "Japan Cancel's Emperor's Birthday Party." Kandis would remind me later.

The day after my plum gathering fest, two Japanese nationals, both passengers on the Diamond Princess, died. Later, over

3000 infections and 82 deaths would be tracked back to cruise ships: those multi-decked pleasure palaces extolling dream vacations replete with sunny decks, ballrooms, international cuisine, game rooms, spas, pools, and exotic ports of call. Cruise ship employees caught in quarantine limbo and unable to be repatriated back to their home countries pleaded for help from unresponsive governments. More than one, in their desperation, committed suicide.

In class that Saturday, we created Scenes of Arashiyama: river banks with plum trees (although they were supposed to be cherry) and azalea; places where priests and nobles, court ladies and commoners had walked in centuries past to admire blossoms. The area hosts my ikebana school's headquarters: the former summer palace of Emperor Saga, a timeless place where people still walk the banks of the *Oigawa* to revel in the seasonal changes.

For a couple of hours, we forgot about coronavirus news and focused on our Natural Scene arrangements, placing rocks into our *suibans* to create miniature river banks, lining them with plum branches and tucking a little color around the rocks with sprigs of purple winter heather. Life carried on per normal in our part of the world; we thought it always would.

Greedy for more plum branches, I returned a second and third time to the pile awaiting the chipper guys. On my last trip to load up the car, the "machine" had beaten me to it; all the branches were gone. What a sad day that was, to know that those hundreds of plum buds would not be able to fulfill their destiny and be admired by every passing motorist. There should be an ordinance about such things. No chipping budded branches before they've bloomed.

Later, as the news began to pour out of Asia and into the US, the plum blossoms that never got to bloom seemed all the more poignant—lives cut short, livelihoods ended. Spring had brought with it more than cheerful reminders of renewal, hope and endurance; it had brought its dark side. The coronavirus had silently sailed to America; it had been circulating for a month, maybe longer. Before the end of February, our state would become the epicenter of the SARS Cov-2 pandemic. But only a mere one week prior, the coronavirus felt far away and non-threatening. Yes, it was in the news; the virus rampaged through Iran and South Korea; but having no experience with pandemics, I, and millions of other Americans, couldn't wrap our minds around the threat that it would become. Even though Japan issued a travel warning on February 24, I still thought our trip to Japan would happen on April 1.

All the while I'd been planning several ikebana events in Seattle, and that was mostly on my mind. As a member of Ikebana International, I had volunteered to do the weekly arrangement at the newly reopened and renovated Asian Art Museum; that same week the Northwest Flower and Garden Show at Seattle's Convention Center hosted an ikebana show and demonstration by the fifth-generation Ohara ikebana master from Japan Hiroki Ohara. He would not only perform a traditional demonstration at the Convention Center but an innovative performance at Benaryoya Hall called "Ikebana X Technology: Japanese Flower Art Meets Mixed Reality."

The day before leaving for Seattle, a text message from Kandis said, "Can you talk?"

The ensuing conversation began with, "Do you think we should cancel our trip?"

Hmm! Cancel our trip....

It ended with, "See if we can get a refund."

I knew that our tickets said "non-refundable," so in my mind I imagined Kandis calling the airlines, the airlines denying a refund, and, not wanting to lose the price of a plane ticket, we'd talk again in order to ponder our choices: cancel and lose $1200, or proceed with our trip, ready or not.

By the first day of my ikebana fest in Seattle (February 26), two residents of a Life Care Center in the Kirkland suburb where I was staying died of COVID-19. (Although no one knew the cause at the time.) Still, because of a young man in the next county who returned from Wuhan and tested positive, health authorities advised everyone to "wash hands" frequently, and "don't touch your face." Without understanding the true threat and nature of the virus (the aerosols and droplets), that week saw lots of hand-washing *only* as life continued per normal with thousands of unmasked attendees milling about the Convention Center, shopping for bulbs, plants, kitchen gadgets, garden art, ceramics, cards, paintings, prints, mops: all the "non-essentials." And when the throngs weren't shopping, we were packed inside seminar rooms by the hundreds, or jostling to see the dozens of model landscapes displayed with pots of live trees, tulips, daffodils, shrubs, waterfalls, courtyards, patios…, all of it trucked into the Convention Center by hundreds of vendors and volunteers for this annual plant/flower/spring extravaganza; all of it indoors, no one wearing masks, no one at a distance.

Seated shoulder to shoulder with hundreds of spectators, both ikebana events gave attendees a taste of modern and traditional Japanese ikebana movements, and sent us away awe inspired and giddy knowing that we too, as teachers and students and lovers of Japanese culture, partook in this ancient art form. We felt carefree then, unconcerned. How quickly life changed. The day of the Ikebana X Technology event, Japan's Prime Minister, Shinzo Abe, took the unprecedented move of closing all schools.

That night a telephone call announced: "Got a full refund. The flight change thing."

"Really?"

Shocked by the finality of our canceled trip and how it too transpired so quickly, the new reality set in that, after months and months of pre-trip planning, Kandis, Robert and I would *not* be spending April in Kyoto. Still in Kirkland on February 28, with free time between the two ikebana events, I spent all day trying to connect with an airline agent.

Back in January an email from the airlines informed us that our "non-stop" flight from Osaka back to Seattle had been changed to a "one-stop" flight rerouted through Honolulu. Indignant over the inconvenience, but determined to restore our "non-stop" flight, we cut one day off our itinerary. Fast forward two months with a pandemic about to overtake the world, with all international flights either canceled or quarantined, and the thing that triggered our refund was not the threat of a deadly virus infecting millions, but the little Honolulu snafu. That next day, just a couple of miles away, and unbeknownst to me and other Washingtonians, a man in his 50s died of COVID-19. More cases proved positive at the nursing home, and the newspapers reported that *nobody on staff knew what hit them*. By the time they did, 36 more residents would die.

Life's uncertainties couldn't have been more tangible. Impermanence glared its grin of self-righteousness. The masters had been warning us for eons, "don't cling to anything."

Plum branches with camellia
Original container by Reid Ozaki

After my whirlwind ikebana trip in the "big city," I returned home in cancelation mode: inn in Kyoto, hotel in Kanazawa, *shukubo* at Koyasan, lunch at Tenryuji, shuttle from airport. I crossed off "make train reservations to Mt. Yoshino," emailed my flower temple correspondent, Rev. Tomomatsu, that we wouldn't be coming to Japan; emailed my Reiki teacher; and in a surge of foolish optimism happily announced to my students that we could now have ikebana classes in April.

Two days later, the number of infected people in the US had doubled. On March 7, we had 279 cases, 102 of them in my home state of Washington. By the middle of the week the World Health Organization called the new coronavirus a global pandemic. The same day, the president issued an order blocking all European travelers to the US. Washington State became the first US epicenter.

Sitting at my computer wondering what now, I eyed the nine packets of cosmos seeds on my desk, seeds I'd ordered the previous year from an online retailer after our visit to Hannyaji, the Cosmos Temple in Nara. That trip in 2018 could have been another beginning to this story, a time when the flower temple pilgrimage became a bit more tangible, a little more than an idea percolating in my creative brain. On that trip, the Cosmos Temple, a taster "flower temple," and maybe the last taste I would ever get, was one of many events scheduled on our itinerary. The main reason for going to Japan in October of that particular year, rather than November when the maple leaves are stunning, or April, when the cherry blossoms are stunning, was to celebrate 1200 years of history at Daikakuji temple. On that trip we partook in an ikebana workshop taught by a Saga master, viewed an ikebana exhibit attended by Japanese royalty, and, more importantly participated in a special ceremony to honor Emperor Saga's Heart Sutra copy only revealed once every 60 years.

Heart Sutra copying, or *shakyo*, appeared in Japan as a religious devotional practice in the eighth century; it was also one way, pre-printing press, of spreading the teachings of Buddha to everyone. Emperors engaged in the practice for the good of the people and the country. During the reign of Emperor Saga, a serious smallpox epidemic plagued the land. The monk Kukai (posthumously Kobo Daishi) suggested that the Emperor copy the Heart Sutra with the intention of alleviating the epidemic. Emperor Saga, like other Emperors, brushed the Heart Sutra in gold ink on indigo paper. The gold ink symbolizes the light of Buddha radiating out into the world. The epidemic stopped; and Emperor Saga's Heart Sutra has been preserved in a special tabernacle at Daikakuji Temple ever since.

Copying the Heart Sutra, still a devotional prayer practice even today, is meant to create a field of "merit" or positive karma; this is then offered to dispel a person's or nation's "suffering" of disease, misfortune, calamity, or what have you. Each kanji character emits the light of compassionate intent for as long as the ink remains to be seen; thus the wisdom of the Heart Sutra still touches people today, still works to dispel negativity in the world. Our times, like their times, are not unique. These times, like their times, are the ever-changing landscape of human suffering with a modern twist: *we* can avoid isolation via Zoom; *we* might get a vaccine.

On March 13, 2020, the president signed the "Proclamation on Declaring a National Emergency Concerning the Novel Coronavirus Disease (COVID-19) Outbreak." He had already suspended entry of foreign nationals from China, Iran and some parts of Europe, but it was too little, too late. The virus had been spreading in the US for months. Our "national emergency"— more than a virus we would soon discover—had been creeping up on us for a long time—for decades, centuries in fact, even though these layers of crises were yet to be revealed.

The next day, in an act of resignation or forced optimism, I planted the cosmos seeds in little peat pots and placed them in my office window. By late summer/early fall I hoped to have armloads of cosmos for my own arrangements, and my students (more foolish optimism).

The seeds, already two years old, had been sitting behind my computer throughout heat and cold, for going on two years. Germination was a gamble. But within five days of placing those little brown slivers in potting soil and giving them a little water, the late spring sun coaxed them into the light and tiny green sprouts emerged.

Even though seeds are planted, dropped, or blown by the wind every day, every year, creating crops, trees, weeds, wildflowers and everything else, seeing those hard-sided skinny little things disappear under a quarter inch of soil only to materialize as green sprouts five days later, seemed absolutely improbable. Yet the ease with which they germinated should be a lesson for us all: be aware of what you plant, be it thought, word or deed.

I had Velouette; Bright Lights; Versailles Flush; Candy Stripe; Daydream; Versailles Red; Rubinato; Xanthos; and Sonata White. Reading their names and the brilliant colors they represented felt like reading a menu at a gourmet restaurant. My eyes salivated.

By the middle of March, as Governor Inslee prepared Washingtonians for, "Stay Home, Stay Healthy," I sent a less enthusiastic email to my students, "Ikebana classes are canceled until further notice." Now I'd have plenty of time to water my seedlings and watch them grow; plenty of time to pick up my Heart Sutra copying practice; plenty of time for meditating, writing, creating; plenty of time for all the things I thought I never had enough time for.

In *A Zen Wave: Basho's Haiku and Zen*, Aitken Roshi recalls Dogen's question: "Without bitterest cold that penetrates to the very bone, how can plum blossoms spill forth their fragrance all over the world?"

What would be the "fragrance" of this time of "bitter cold"? In March, 2020, with numbers of infected rising and death tolls mounting, with businesses closing, food bank lines growing longer and the unemployed heading into millions, I couldn't yet smell anything sweet. And we, as a country, didn't know it in March, but that "sweet fragrance" would evade us for a very long time.

Chapter 2

Daffodil in the Time of COVID

blooming flowers —
residents of this world, too,
for a short time
Issa

Tendai Buddhists hold the view that poetry, literature, the arts and all creative paths are to be embraced as avenues to enlightenment. "All things are seen as dharma. Rather than distractions, the arts are seen as vehicles toward truth."

Saicho, the monk who brought Tendai Buddhism to Japan from China, coined the phrase "Light up your Corner," which means "changing the world begins with sharing your unique gifts with the world, starting where you are. By lighting up your own corner of the world, you light up the whole world."

My imagined "flower temple pilgrimage," meant to renew a twenty-five-year practice of ikebana, and a deepening journey of Kado: The Way of Flowers, had an original subtext of inspiring others to take up ikebana for inner peace and ultimately world peace — a light in the world. More than merely sticking an assortment of colorful blooms in a vase, ikebana brought one closer to the rhythms of nature, to forms and the absence of forms, to the yin and yang of opposing forces, and to the pure heart of flowers in deep and satisfying ways. A master of the Koryu School, Zeshinken Ichiro, said that he "sought to encounter flowers on a deep level and undertake the beauty concealed within... cultivating the spirit is the greatest purpose of flower arranging."

His truth resurrected mine: the path of Kado, an artistic route to being in the present moment, to waking up, a path in line with the Buddhist vows I'd started preparing for—vows that included, "maintaining creative practice and activity in the arts," (unique to the Order of Ryokan). The Way of Flowers, a "moving" Zen practice, and meditation a "sitting" Zen practice, grounded body and spirit. What would it look like if Kado *was* a path to enlightenment? It might look like being as poised, unself-conscious, pure, delicate and unafraid as a flower—a thing of beauty that has no sense of clinging to its beauty, its specialness, its uniqueness or anything that smacks of self-importance and permanence. There's no ideology coming from a flower—no opinions, no stances of right or wrong, good or bad—only the purity of being simple, uncomplicated yet magically complex, and holy, in a way. You wouldn't think to be rough or coarse with a flower. Quite the contrary! Flowers make people happy and gentle; they make them smile.

Ikebana acted as a bridge between humankind and nature, yet it took me to the age of 40 to discover that "bridge," to own my artistic unfolding; and it took nearly to the age of 70 to validate the art of ikebana as a Way. Out of this hard-won sense of validation I could now recommend ikebana to others as a viable path to understanding the True Self. When one works with flowers—observes, grows, and studies flowers—and contemplates how they are born, bloom, die and regenerate, one comes closer to understanding the natural rhythms of all life, a human life outside of ego identity. "Cultivate the spirit," said Ichiro-san. Flower arranging for awakening felt like a worthy corner to keep lit.

Flower design, or "living flowers," (aka ikebana) had been gifted to me by my teacher, Mary Hiroko Shigaya; and when she died, Nobuko Ohgi carried the torch forward by presiding over the Saga School in Seattle. I aspired to leave a corner of this ikebana light in the world, as they had done. I wanted others to cross the bridge, to connect with the positive energy of flowers, an energy that allowed no room for negativity, and provided a respite from suffering and turmoil, sadness, grief and outrage. For someone practicing ikebana and Buddhism for the last twenty-five years, "flowers" and "temples"—a "flower temple pilgrimage"—had sounded like a winning combination.

"A flower does not talk," says Zenkei Shibayama in his book of the same name, but what a flower conveys in silence has captivated the imagination of poets, artists and philosophers for centuries. And yet, have we been listening of late? What can a mere flower—delicate, beautiful, pure, a thing associated with feminine characteristics—say to us now, at this time, and this place? What could a "flower temple" call us to do, remember, or reflect upon?

Life, as always, had the last word; it presented its own secret design. Still, what remained, whether traveling to flower temples or staying home, was a flower's calming magic; its ability to dissipate bad moods and harmful thoughts. Many times, unpleasant feelings or general irritations transformed upon the magic touch of hand to flower. Now in the time of COVID, flowers' "calming magic" was needed more than ever. *Be with nature, notice the flowers*; it's a child's idea, an innocent idea, which is why I liked it so much. It's not complicated; it doesn't require an elaborate manual, a workshop with endless instructions, a degree in anything. Just everybody, drop what you're doing—especially you with the gun—find some lovely flowers, or a branch, leaf, or twig, and create something. Stroll through a garden. Create a garden. Visit a garden; maybe even a flower temple garden in Japan if you have the chance.

Daffodil with dogwood

The long-awaited daffodil season had finally arrived on the mountain even though the little charmers had been blooming for over a month on the mainland, and at least two weeks in the lowlands. Daffodil, one of the "four friends of snow" or "three auspicious flowers that celebrate spring," appeal on many levels. In my world they are bright, cheerful, arrive when it's still technically winter, grow anywhere with little or no care or any great soil, and deer don't eat them, (critical on an island over-populated with hungry doe, fawn and buck). Just looking at the perfect little nodding faces of early blooming Jetfire, a dwarf Cyclamineus daffodil with dark yellow petals and a reddish-orange trumpet, gave one a feeling of hope. In Japan, the daffodil is akin to a "divine announcement," proclaiming the revelation of spring.

With nearly the whole country in lockdown and all restaurants, gift shops, bakeries, libraries, museums, hotels, B&Bs, Airbnbs, and bars shuttered on our little island, the time to fertilize and compost around my daffodils, and all the other bulbs and perennials poking through the soil, could no longer be avoided. Hardware stores and nurseries, considered "essential" businesses, provided the necessary soil amendments. On a blue tarp out by the well, last year's compost heap awaited newly bought bags of chicken manure and boxes of cottonseed and alfalfa meal. Wheelbarrow and digger claw in hand, off I went resigned to "Stay Home, Stay Healthy," and stay busy. I started in the septic area, a plot of earth where I wanted to hide the two green septic tank lids and the white alarm box. The mugo pines had finally grown large enough to hide the lids, and the rest of the area provided plenty of space for irises, crocosmia, lilies, peonies and daffodils. I dumped bucket after bucket of compost around the perennials and evened it out with my digger claw. But in my haste to mix in fertilizer around a clump of miniature Jetfire darlings, I accidentally, and unwittingly decapitated a few..., well, five, no less. Those little yellow and orange faces lay on the ground reflecting back a nation and a world that literally didn't know what hit them. Saddened... no, mortified; I cradled their heads in the palm of my hand.

Daffodils and jonquils, all members of *Narcissus*, a species originating in the Mediterranean region, procured the name we use via Greek mythology. Narcissus was known for his beauty, and also for his haughty ways with women. After snubbing the nymph Echo, Nemesis, the goddess of revenge, decided to punish him. She led him to a clear pond where he saw for the first time his own reflection. Taking his reflection for another, he mistakenly fell in love with himself. When he realized his error, he became distraught and committed suicide.

I prefer the Japanese name for Narcissus, *suisen*, which

means "water hermit," or the Chinese name *shui-hsien*, "water goddess," a reference to the tiny blooms poking up through spring rains and melting snow. On Awaji Island, *suisen tazetta*, a fragrant daffodil with a corona reminiscent of a wine cup (*tazza* in Italian) naturalize freely and bloom in the thousands. They evoke rebirth and new beginnings.

I had planted my little Jetfire bulbs three autumns ago. They were the perfect humble little flower hermits for Natural Scene ikebana arrangements. Each spring without fail, after lying under soil and snow, in sub-freezing weather for weeks and months, the longer days coaxed the bulbs out of slumber and darkness toward new growth and cheerful blooms. They shone in their "corner of light" for about three weeks, normally. But this time, wham! Now the bulbs would have to wait a whole long year for their chance to bloom again. They'd been robbed of their full "corner." To redeem myself, and give them their full due, I floated their little heads in the birdbath on my deck. The five of them, looking like ballerinas in yellow tutus, created their own dance, a kind of free-form ikebana where they got to shine for a little while.

Around the time of my accidental daffodil execution, the House and Senate debated the finer details of an economic stimulus package to save the US from total economic meltdown. As unemployment surged into the millions, and airline, restaurant, hotel, and other "non-essential" businesses collapsed, Congress voted in favor of a $2.2 trillion rescue package—yes, House and Senate working together.

In other headlines, New York City doctors described their hospitals as hell realms; and partying Mardi Gras style in the time of COVID produced the headline, "New Orleans Faces a Virus Nightmare." The coronavirus epicenter had spread like a tidal wave from West Coast to East.

As I watched the five little daffodil heads twirling around in the birdbath, I berated myself for not being more mindful, for failing to live the "Zen of movement": awake, aware, present. The decapitated daffodils reminded me of how quickly impermanence manifests, how ones very life can change in a millisecond. The Jetfires, hopeful and joyous on a sunny day, now, having met with a human, had their innocence taken away. This was not a time to be careless or self-absorbed, but a time to be wide-eyed, conscientious, and alert. This was a time, in the Time of COVID, to *not* take anything or anyone for granted, not our friends, neighbors, strangers, and especially not our health care workers, farmers, grocery and retail clerks, mail carriers and other essential workers.

By March 26, a mere one month from mingling with thousands at the Seattle Convention Center and Ikebana shows, the US reported the most coronavirus cases of any country in the world. How did that happen so quickly and unobtrusively?

After three days and nights of rain, my little ballerinas had finished their ballet and folded into two yellow heaps on either side of the birdbath. The pandemic was in full swing. It didn't take long for the island to institute safety measures. Our co-op went to online ordering and curbside pickup only; the supermarket staggered the flow of customers and erected Plexiglas barriers at each cash register. Home deliveries to high-risk populations became common place.

I ordered my first box of groceries through our co-op's website and picked it up the next day. We already had shortages: oatmeal, plain almond yoghurt, unscented laundry detergent. But it was okay, I could adjust. I went to the supermarket. They too had shortages: no vegan bacon, organic hummus, carrot juice or my favorite brand of organic frozen orange and apple juice that I used to sweeten my plain yoghurt. But it was okay, I could adjust. These shortages were not dire, only served to highlight how spoiled I was, how life in America is all about preferences and privilege; how I'd taken dozens of food choices for granted and assumed luxuries were necessities.

In between grocery ordering and yard work, I created flower arrangements with daffodils: crabapple branches with daffodil, pine and daffodil, spirea and daffodil; until the rain beat down most of the early bloomers.

Headlines continued to stun the world with reports of COVID cases in unexpected places: Prime Minister Boris Johnson, Tom Hanks, Rita Wilson, Prince Charles. No one was spared. China suspended foreign travelers as they worried about a second wave. And when unemployment reached 3 million Americans (we thought that a staggering number at the time), I vowed not to whine about "shortages."

It snowed twice the first week of April. By then late blooming daffodils began to open—along with primroses, pansies, red-flowering currant and forsythia. The nation was asking, *Should we be wearing face masks?* after we'd been told for months that we didn't need them—even though people in China, South Korea, and Japan had been wearing masks from the beginning.

The UK Prime Minister was admitted to the ICU; the US reported over 10,000 deaths; and Dr. Anthony Fauci, our pandemic guru, became a target of online conspiracy theorists.

The world facing a pandemic, a time of cooperation you'd think, opposing sides working together, the federal government helping the states—you know, "team spirit." But it was quite the opposite. With so many angry, desperate, fearful people unemployed—all of them gun owners—a tension hung over the country, one that would explode in unexpected ways in the Time of Peony.

The only brightness in my world, the one that offered respite from the unrelenting coronavirus news was the hundreds of daffodils that continued to bloom along the nearly deserted streets in town, and the dozens still blooming in my yard. But after more rains, even they were looking a little weary as heads began to hang, stems bent or broke, and the early ones packed it up until next year. Next year... a future time, a time when life might return to normal, felt unimaginable, dreamlike, a wild fantasy.

Chapter 3

Cherry Blossom in the Time of COVID

what a strange thing!
to be alive
beneath cherry blossoms
Issa

No other culture that I know of observes nature as keenly, precisely, and with such poetic sensitivity as the Japanese. Cherry blossoms are not merely cherry blossoms; the Japanese have defined 11 steps in the flowering of cherry trees: budding, swelling, blooming, flowering 10%, 30%, 50%, 70%, full bloom, decline, petal fall, and late flowering. Iconic, clichéd, beloved: the first official *hanami*, or cherry blossom festival was thought to be held in Kyoto 1200 years ago by Emperor Saga, the founding inspiration behind my ikebana school: Saga Goryu.

Every year, Japan puts out a Cherry Blossom Forecast: predictions of when and where revelers can expect to see the various stages of cherry blossoms. In 2020, the season came early to Kyoto: March 23; the same date that launched our state's "Stay Home, Stay Healthy" directive. In the time of our own country's cherry blossom season, New York became the new epicenter of the pandemic and experienced the highest "attack rate" of any place in the world; at their peak over 600 people died every day from COVID-19.

While the virus spread to every corner of the globe, ceasefires would be called upon by the UN Secretary-General, Antonio Guterres. He would say, "End the sickness of war and fight the disease that is ravaging our world." Could this pandemic bring an end to world conflict? To war? Although several countries pledged support for Guterres' appeal, very few implemented them. In Yemen, conflicts spiked. Libya, although initially welcoming the idea, experienced escalating clashes. In Afghanistan, the violence continued per usual. Only Syria maintained a ceasefire, at least for awhile.

In the time of cherry blossoms, a YouTube video called #LISTEN came through my Facebook feed. The language: Italian; the message: "from the virus"; the voice: feminine and compelling, narrated a series of images depicting human impact on earth: the impending catastrophe of the Sixth Extinction: massive fires, melting glaciers, rampant pollution of air, water and land. "We are all suffering," said the soft persuasive voice. "We are not okay." Film footage in fast motion depicted the unceasing activity of humans: building, flying, driving, consuming, polluting... The voice said, "Look at the earth. How is she doing?" The message from the virus implied that it took this drastic measure of a global pandemic to stop humans from our destructive behaviors. Now to save our lives and the lives of others, our sheer fear of death compelled us to stay in place. We've canceled flights, trips, outings. Air pollution in Bejing and New Delhi, LA and New York, has literally blown away. A woman wearing a mask appeared on the screen. The voice said, "Learn to smile with your eyes. I'm here to help. Just listen."

According to the World Health Organization, deaths related to air pollution top 7 million annually. Their website says, "Nine out of ten people breathe air containing high levels of pollutants." Already, an emergency of "breathing" had crept into the world, and "I Can't Breathe" moved ever closer into our consciousness.

In the beginning of the pandemic, in the Time of Cherry Blossoms, the truth of the virus' message could not be disputed. Only a world crisis "literally taking our breath away" had made us take stock of our habits: all the "stuff" we thought we had to have; all the places we thought we had to go; all the goods we thought we had to consume. Our nation suddenly had trillions of dollars to keep the economy from total collapse, but had never had enough for the homeless, the hungry or the uninsured. "Where does all this money come from?" a friend asked, bewildered. "They print it," I said. "Borrow it from banks, investors, bonds."

"Who understands any of this?"

"Somebody does."

And yet, we don't. We don't know how to spread the wealth around, how to provide health care for all, how to keep people from losing their homes, how to stop our march toward the cliff of mass extinction and global environmental catastrophe, how to slow down climate change. Or perhaps we did know, but lacked the will, lacked generosity, cooperation and a shared vision to implement the necessary actions.

These words of Sekkei Harada startled me, yet I knew they were true, "[A]s long as there is no co-existence or mutual support among people [human]kind will become extinct in the twenty-first century." The signs were everywhere.

In the face of our world meltdown, cherry blossom season would continue as an innocent witness to human folly; its dispassionate presence, whether in Japan, or here, or anywhere, mattered little to the virus. But for a few brief weeks in April, cherry blossoms would relieve some of our angst; it was a certainty, a phenomenon that could alleviate complete despair. Despite human mishaps, miscalculations, injustice and stupidity, iconic cherry blossom season would come again and again, year after year, starting in March and ending in April, for as long as there were cherry trees and those who loved them. Nature is unstoppable. Seasons cycle around, from cherry blossoms to wisteria, to peonies, iris, lotus, chrysanthemum and camellia—virus or not. If we humans, through uncontrollable population and consumption, eliminate ourselves from the earthly equation, cherry blossom season will go on without us. Until that time, we expected that maybe next year, there would be another *Hanami,* a time to celebrate cherry blossoms. But in 2020, thousands of rose budded trees would swell, bloom, decline and fall without a single admirer. Parks, temples, arboretums, riverside promenades, botanical gardens, night-time displays... would all close in keeping with the worldwide "lockdowns."

By the time my little cosmos seedlings reached three inches, Prime Minister Narendra Modi had ordered all 1.3 billion Indian citizens to stay home. India under a 21-day lockdown? Unimaginable! Three days later, the president signed the $2.2 trillion rescue package into law as US coronavirus cases surged and the economy shut down despite all his attempts to control the uncontrollable.

Two weeks into "Stay Home, Stay Healthy," my cosmos seedlings had grown quite gangly. The seedlings literally stretched to find the light, as we were all doing; especially now in the shades of gray that had become our world. The rarest cosmos, Bright Lights, an orange, yellow and gold variety; in defiance of its name wasn't doing well. Versailles Red, although leggy, looked promising. I moved the seedlings into the brighter living room and waited for them to develop a set of "true" leaves, the time to pinch the end to induce branching. Perhaps by summer or early fall my students could return to class and create ikebana with my garden full of cosmos? My optimism, or lack of "clear seeing," seemed to know no bounds.

Four days before our scheduled flight to Japan, a *New York Times* headline gave me pause: "Japan's Virus Success Has Puzzled the World." Was our worry about being packed into Japanese trains and buses, face to face with millions of commuters wearing surgical masks, a real concern, or a needless worry? In that moment it looked like "needless worry"; it looked like we'd be safer in Japan than our own country. Still, even with Japan's "success," all cherry blossom venues would say "canceled" on their websites. Had there ever been such a thing in recorded history? I couldn't imagine Mt. Yoshino with its 30,000 cherry trees, unvisited, unseen.

April 1, the day of our canceled flight to Japan, I glanced at the 72 Season App I'd downloaded during my trip planning enthusiasm. Season #12 announced, "Thunder Raises Its Voice." "When the cherry blossoms are past their prime, sound of thunder... once again begins to rumble in the distant sky. Snowfall can be seen... a reminder amidst the changeable weather that spring is still in early stages."

Cherry blossoms had not yet moved past their prime in my part of the world, but true to the Almanac's ancient wisdom, unseasonal snowflakes began piling up on my deck and onto the primroses that I'm always enticed to buy too early. Everything in the world felt out of whack, upside down, science fiction. Snow in April? Not unheard of, but rare in this part of North America.

Cities around the world, emptied of cars, taxis, motorcycles and buses, experienced clean air for the first time in decades. In Venice, with water taxis shut down, canals became clear again.

My "desk" *senryu:*

April Fool's Day—
our eleven-hour flight
to see sakura

Written, not in the present moment, but months earlier, the poem took on new layers of meaning. Conjured in my imagination and meant to poke fun at two types of "fools": "fools enamored with cherry blossoms," (me) who would gladly endure an 11-hour flight (and who would do that "gladly" with security lines, terrible food, hard chairs and hairy arms on the armrest); and "fools in love," with beauty, the fleeting, and the ephemeral, and all the usual clichéd symbolism of cherry blossoms that drive millions to groves, gardens, and parties to celebrate in the realm of cherry blossom magic. Now, as the pandemic began to reveal all the failures of our society, several new strains of "fool" came to the fore: "fools of privilege," contributing for decades to the smog that now had begun to lift; "unquestioning fools," having been unable to confront the consequences of our own consumer habits; "attached fools," wanting/needing/expecting international travel to be our right and privilege; "fools of denial," thinking we could carry on like this when the planet was suffocating from the burning of fossil fuel emissions; "irresponsible fools," believing someone would eventually solve this problem before it was too late; and, after seeing the documentary *Planet of the Humans*, I added, "delusional fools," convinced that new technologies would save us from ourselves. Later, in the Time of Peony, I would add, "fools of unwitting injustice," for not owning up to racial inequality for centuries.

But in the Time of Cherry Blossoms, my hang-up was "attachment." Attachment being what it is, for a moment I fantasized about other modes of travel so that I wouldn't have to give up my regular trips to Japan. Could I do a Greta Thunberg and hop aboard someone's 60-foot sailboat? Recalling the movie *Adrift*, a harrowing true-life story of survival in the midst of an unforeseen typhoon in the Pacific Ocean..., well, I put that idea on hold.

Cruise ships? Yikes! Would anyone sign up for one of those again?

By 10:30 the snow had mostly melted. The anemone I planted last week, unstopped by cold, had a new red bud preparing to open. A few late blooming Pheasant Eye daffodils out by the well looked undaunted by cold and snow. The cherry blossoms, having bloomed early during our one week of unseasonal warm weather, had already started shedding petals. Insects and micro-organisms that make up the under story, the earth itself, would all benefit. Everything continuously circled around.

On April 2, when I would have been checking into my efficiency apartment near Kitano Tenmangu Shrine in NW Kyoto, the US reported over 200,000 citizens infected with the coronavirus: 4896 in my home state and 74,000 in New York. More than 6.5 million Americans applied for unemployment benefits.

Dr. Anthony Fauci, who put in sixteen-hour days informing the president, the media, Congress and everybody else in the world about what to do and not do in the face of this pandemic, needed security guards to protect his life. Apparently, a few people out there didn't enjoy hearing the truth; didn't "believe" in pandemics; didn't want to "social distance"; didn't want anyone telling them what to do; didn't like scientists contradicting or correcting the president's press briefings; didn't buy what the medical experts advised; still bought the conspiracy theory that Democrats had concocted yet another plot to bring down the president.

Gun and ammunition sales surged—considered an "essential service" for some deranged reason; and alcohol consumption increased despite health experts proclaiming that alcohol compromises our immune system—the last thing you want with a deadly virus roaming around.

Within a month, the US had gone from a Level 1:"Practice usual precautions," to a Level 4: "Do not travel." Our county council advised islanders to avoid trips to the mainland, and to quarantine for 14 days if we had to make an "essential" trip.

Oil prices plummeted and Whiting Petroleum Corporation, the hydraulic fracturing, or "fracking" giant in North Dakota, Montana and Colorado, filed bankruptcy.

Was this the shift away from fossil fuels we'd all been waiting for but didn't know how to achieve? Has it been brought about by some benevolent force for our own good?

Transformation can be gradual, or sudden. And it looked like we were in the thick of "sudden" — ready or not. Nobody said that planetary change would come easy, and nobody except for a handful of pandemic experts, could have conceived of it happening like this.

But life can shift in either direction like an April weather front: one day reveling in cherry blossoms and the next day watching snow falling on your newly planted primroses. One day moving to an island, the next day moving off, the next day staying for ever. The mind shifts with the seasons, with imagined needs/wants/desires.

Isolated on a mountain on an island, I reflected on the many times I'd tried to move off this island, and failed; all the times I ignored Zen wisdom and thought there was something "out there" that was better than "right here." There was the time I wanted to move to a neighboring island; the time I wanted to move back to the town where I went to college; the town between two exciting cities; the town where my Zen teacher lives; the town in another state where it was sunnier, cheaper, livelier... or something. Now all those failures to move felt like a blessing, felt like Shantideva saying, I told you so, didn't I say find a "forest... with birds and deer who say nothing unpleasant..." (a place far removed from mainland turmoil).

By April 3, the day we were to begin our cherry blossom viewing — Kodai-ji, Nanzen-ji, Honen-in, Shoren-in — coronavirus cases exceeded 1 million worldwide, and 10 million Americans had lost their job.

On April 4, the day scheduled to see the spectacular display of cherry trees at Mt. Yoshino, the US reported 277,205 confirmed cases of COVID-19 — the highest of any country in the world.

The news, grim, depressing, and heartbreaking, told of people lying in hospital beds hooked up to ventilators without family and friends at their bedside; loved ones dying alone, saying goodbye via Facetime. Funeral directors in New York, already overwhelmed with the number of corpses, limited the number of people who could attend end of life memorials.

I thumbed through our Japan itinerary, looking for a little relief from CNN, *The New York Times*, NPR, PBS and all the other news sources streaming through computer, phone and radio. I needed a fantasy, an escape. Ah, Mt. Yoshino, one of the most sacred pilgrimage sites in Japan; it would have been our destination on a day like today: spring, sunny, warm. In that other part of the world, the one now in my dreams, cherry trees planted by pilgrims over the last 1200 years would be blossoming successively and continuously from the bottom of the mountain to the top. We would have arrived by train, walked through town, taken a cable car to the top, and paid a visit to Kinpusen-ji Temple, the head temple of the Shugendo sect: a Buddhist-Shinto-Shamanic sect known for mountain ascetic practices. We would have had a healthy Japanese lunch in a hillside restaurant, and afterwards a bowl of matcha with perhaps a cherry blossom inspired confection; maybe a light pink mochi wrapped in a salted cherry leaf.

I thought of cherry trees as offerings: gifts of thanks to the *kami* or mountain spirits, to the Divine Mother; a pilgrim's heartfelt contribution to the beauty and splendor of a magnificent holy site. What a blessing to plant a cherry tree on a sacred mountain!

On the island, we didn't have the likes of a Mt. Yoshino where Shinto shrines and Buddhist temples had welcomed pilgrims and priests for over a thousand years. We didn't have temples, dharma centers, or Japanese gardens. What we had on our island was a row of double pink cherry trees across the parking lot from the Senior Center, a few singles along Main Street, one in the Episcopalian church yard, a friend's orchard.... For inspiration, I googled Kinpusen-ji, our final destination on Mt. Yoshino, and clicked "translate into English."

Kii Mountains have been worshipped as a place where gods dwell from the mythological era, but under the influence of the newly

introduced Buddhism, it becomes a stage for mountain training to
acquire the mysterious power hidden in the universe and nature...

"Mysterious power" indeed! Nature: spellbinding in its many manifestations; mysterious in its invisible workings; enigmatic in how it has captured the heart and soul of humans since the beginning of time; would nature have the last say?

Before I could contemplate an answer, my phone bleeped, "Breaking News": "Virus spikes in Japan."

In the week between Palm Sunday and Easter, we, as a nation were predicted to reach the apex of the COVID-19 pandemic, with record deaths and massive hospitalizations that would overwhelm our health care system. It was also, according to the ancient Japanese almanac, the Season of Clear and Bright, a time for spring outings to wild places, a time when swallows and geese return from the north, a time to gather fiddlehead bracken fern for soups. In light of the depressing news, and the desire to offer something uplifting for our friends, my sister and I began cleaning up our forest labyrinth, and the paths leading to it. With "Stay Home, Stay Healthy" we needed projects, distractions, creative outlets. Our intention was to invite friends over, one person or household at a time in keeping with social distancing, to walk the labyrinth Easter weekend, the official weekend of light and rebirth. The labyrinth was our very own "temple garden" of sorts—not one filled with fabulous flowers, but of various native plants like *Prunella vulgaris* or commonly called self-heal or heart-of-the-earth; *Mahonia nervosa* (Oregon grape); *Rosa gymnocarpa* (wild rose); several kinds of fern; and most importantly, *Bryophyte*, or moss—lots of thick bright green moss.

We had created the labyrinth ten years ago after a Zen sesshin at a retreat center in Arizona. Our labyrinth, modeled after the Center's rock labyrinth, had 11 circuits, the same style found at Chartres Cathedral in France, except that ours was in the "cathedral of the forest" on the mountain, on the island where we lived. We had created the paths using small stones found around the property — buckets and buckets of stones. We lined the pathways with the rocks in the 11-circuit shape, all measured precisely by my sister Gwen. The rocks had to be small enough to create the desired design within the circular shape we found on our forested land, a natural circle surrounded by tall fir trees. The deer liked to walk through the labyrinth, and between their hooves and our clumsy feet the little rocks often got displaced and had to be realigned. On occasion a tree would come down in a storm and fall near or across the labyrinth. We'd have to ask our neighbor to come over with his chainsaw to cut it up into fireplace logs. Now we had a pile of neatly stacked firewood beside the labyrinth.

Overtime, the moss had grown up and over the rocks that created the lines of the path, so that now, we had a moss labyrinth, the kind you might see at Saijo-ji Temple in Kyoto — if they were ever inclined to make labyrinths out of moss, which they haven't to date. We no longer needed the rocks, and most of them were buried under the moss.

But here's the thing, if you don't walk the labyrinth — as had become our state of taking something sacred for granted — the moss grows into the path itself, *obscuring* it. The labyrinth had always evoked endless metaphors and this one became quite obvious the day I went out to clean it up for our upcoming event. The path, literally and figuratively, had to be walked, had to be experienced and maintained, and not neglected.

Joko Beck says, "We need an adequate daily period of zazen in which we attend to what's going on in our minds and bodies."

Buddhists in Japan had taken their sacred spaces for granted; many temples, unvisited, fell to neglect. The priests tried to resurrect them, to make them relevant again; they sought to enhance their sacred spaces with flowers — flowers to lure people into sacred space, because we lived in an age where we had to be coaxed and cajoled into the holy interiors of our own being.

One day while cleaning up the labyrinth, I found what appeared to be an Indian arrowhead. I didn't know if it was an *authentic* arrowhead, but it made me ponder who might have lived on or visited the mountain in centuries past. The islands had been home to the Coast Salish people for over 8000 years. Their populations declined rapidly after Spanish explorers, traders and trappers brought viruses from their home countries, viruses where the native populations had no immunity, viruses that killed: smallpox, chickenpox, measles. These diseases had been circulating among humans for centuries; and, like COVID-19, if you've never been exposed and had no antibodies—a state of affairs called "virgin soil effect"—you could die, just like millions of indigenous people had died.

Finding the arrowhead lying next to the labyrinth path connected the past to the present. Pandemic was not new; epidemics, and viruses that kill were as old as Homo sapiens. We, in the twenty-first century, were not special.

By April 7 Japan declared a state of emergency. The virus that they thought had been eradicated, re-surfaced. We had been scheduled to visit the 1000 cherry trees at Daigo-ji Temple made famous by Hideyoshi Toyotomi's infamous cherry blossom viewing parties. Then as now, this was a time when friends and family lay blankets on the grass under cherry trees to eat, drink and be merry, celebrating with abandon the iconic symbol of divine impermanence, fleeting beauty and our short stay on Mother Earth.

The next day, April 8, Buddha's Birthday, a day for viewing late blooming Omuro cherry trees at Ninnanji in Kyoto, the US experienced the highest daily death toll in one day: nearly 2000.

On the mountain, as we readied for several friends to partake in our Easter Day Labyrinth Event—a time to light a candle, a stick of incense and walk the "sacred path"—two more positive cases showed up on the island: a couple who ran a popular farm stand. Seeing how quickly and unobtrusively the virus spread and infected the unsuspecting, fearing the potential for exposure that wouldn't reveal results for up to two weeks, we pondered the wisdom of inviting others into the unknown territory of "community-spread." The risk might have been minimal, but any risk if it endangered our friends felt like too much. We canceled the event.

Instead of participating in a sacred nature ritual with friends, at a time representative of resurrection and renewal, of light and courage, I spent another day "Staying Home, Staying Healthy," and watching YouTube: a video of blossoming cherry trees at Ninna-ji.

Italy had become the epicenter of the virus with staggering daily death rates. Pope Francis offered words that went beyond the boundaries of the pandemic:

Let us silence the cries of death, no more wars! May we stop the production and trade of weapons, since we need bread, not guns. May the hearts of those who have enough be open to filling the empty hands of those who do not have the bare necessities. May we bring the song of life!

Ah, a fresh breeze of wisdom wafting through a sunny spring day: cherry blossoms letting go, scattering in the wind, replenishing the earth, offering their "song of life."

And at Duomo Cathedral in Milan, Andrea Bocelli, the famous tenor, gave a solo performance called "Music for Hope," singing "Ave Maria," and "Sancta Maria," both songs requesting that Mary, the Mother of God, intervene in the suffering of humans. The plea is universal, the prayer, said in various languages, in various ways, carries the same meaning. Mary, Tara, Guanyin, Kannon, Avalokiteshvara…, please intervene, hear our cry of suffering.

During Bocelli's performance, film footage showing the empty streets of Milan, Paris, London and New York reminded the 38 million viewers that this was no ordinary concert, but one that would live forever in our memories as the time of COVID. We would remember all those who were sick, and all those who died—by that Easter day 20,000 in Italy alone—and we would hope too that this virus would bring Mary's healing for our world, "now and at the time of our death."

For Easter weekend in Kyoto, we had scheduled an outing to Daikaku-ji Temple and my ikebana school's annual floral tribute ceremony. The ritual's purpose is to honor Emperor Saga and bestow gratitude to all the flowers and plant life that gave of themselves for the sake of ikebana throughout the year. This year's flower processions, sutra chanting, and tea ceremonies—all canceled; touring Daikakuji—forbidden; the pond, grounds and temple—closed to the public.

By the end of Easter weekend, cherry blossoms in Kyoto would be past their prime if not gone altogether. We would have seen all the famous cherry viewing spots and scheduled a "down day" to relax and recoup before setting out to see kerria in Nara. Maybe as long as it took carbon dioxide emitting airplanes to get me from here to there, I couldn't justify air travel anymore. I hadn't wanted to confront that before, and didn't think I would have to. Everybody in the developed world flies from here to there; it's natural, unavoidable and, well, our right, right? But the writing was more than on the wall; it was spreading like a virus, unstoppable. The virus from a theoretical bat in a supposed wild animal market in China had found a new host, humans. The underlying cause pointed toward over population, which led to destruction of habitat for food production, which led to capturing more and more wild animals and keeping them caged in unsanitary "wet markets": markets that had been banned in China but kept creeping back in underground.

The month of April, generally a time to celebrate spring in the northern hemisphere instead brought ominous words from the president, *the next two weeks are going to be very, very painful.* The prediction foretold that 100,000 to 240,000 American's could lose their lives to COVID-19, even with social distancing; and without social distancing the number could go as high as 2 million. Food supplies could be threatened if farms couldn't hire skilled workers, and already in some cities, mile-long lines of cars awaited food pickup from food banks. The National Guard, called up to help with food distribution, replaced volunteer positions held by seniors: the high-risk group.

Thoughts of cherry blossoms and daffodils, peonies and wisteria, kerria and chrysanthemum offered respite and relief. I didn't know of any other phenomena other than the beauty of nature—how it unfolds in colorful shapes and sizes, in symmetry and fragrance, in delicate and non-delicate ways, in myriads of variety—that provided such an absolute antidote to despair. I am an ikebana practitioner who lives on a mountain on an island in the midst of a global pandemic. Flowers might not save my life, but they promised to save my sanity.

Cherry blossom with iris

Chapter 4

Kerria in the Time of COVID

a petal shower
of mountain roses,
and the sound of the rapids
Basho

Warmer days soon put *Kerria japonica* or *yamabuki* (mountain rose) into bud stage. The single petal variety, favored over the "fluffy ruffle" kind (botanically named Pleniflora, or pom-pom style), struggled to survive in the midst of encroaching salal that thrived on the mountain. I kept an eye on my two bushes so as not to miss the perfect stage for an ikebana arrangement. In the week after Easter, little promising things like kerria buds opening kept me going.

We had entered Season #15 of the ancient Japanese almanac: "The First Rainbow Appears," but neither literal nor figurative rainbows could be found. On the mountain, our usual April rains held back for over a week; the first time in twelve years. Drought and lack of "rainbows" reflected the continuing bleakness of the news: 17 deaths in one nursing home forced staff to store corpses in a shed; death tallies nationwide escalated; conflicts began between the president and the World Health Organization, the president and Governor Cuomo, the president and Governor Inslee, the president and just about everybody as he proclaimed, "It's going to disappear. One day—it's like a miracle—it will disappear." By late April, the virus hadn't "disappeared," but it had killed another 30,000 Americans, bringing our nation's total to 62,000.

Even in the midst of this staggering number, after peak COVID surge here and abroad, a few glimmers of that illusive, but desperately needed "silver lining" began to emerge: hundreds of dogs and cats confined in animal shelters were being fostered and adopted; views of distant mountains, once obscured by smog, appeared on the horizon; quarantined apartment dwellers in Italy and New York stood on balconies banging pots and pans and cheering on medical workers as they left long grueling shifts.

When to "reopen the economy" became the next big question on everyone's mind as we plunged into unprecedented unemployment. Unsure when I'd ever be able to teach classes again, my attention turned back to *Kerria japonica*. Native to mountainous regions of Japan and China, it too, like *Cosmos bipinnatus* at Hannyaji, the Cosmos Temple, carries symbolic Buddhist meaning. Since the flower does not bear fruit, it is said to have a melancholy feeling, or *mono no aware*, a deep sadness that evokes the fragile beauty of the relative world. Expressed another way, the "Verse of the Diamond Sutra" intones:

A star at dawn
A bubble in a stream
A flash of lightening in a summer cloud
A flickering lamp
A phantom and a dream
So too, this fleeting world.

Because of the transient nature of the delicate kerria flower, it—along with plum, cherry, wisteria, iris and many others— assumes a prominent place in Japanese literature. Favored at a seventh-century Buddhist nunnery in Nara called Chugu- ji, kerria bushes, described in their literature as "stunning," surround the main hall. The temple, thought to have been built for Prince Shotoku's mother, Empress Anahobe-no-Hashihito, houses an elegant Kannon statue said to have an "archaic smile," one of the three great smiles known to the world—the other two being the Great Sphinx and the Mona Lisa. An "archaic smile" implies that the subject lives on with an eternal sense of well-being; thus, this nunnery is said to have maintained "the light of Buddhism for 1300 years." No surprises then that Chugu-ji, although not famous, had been on our Japan itinerary.

In the wild, kerria, with its long arching stems loaded with deep yellow blossoms typically hang over mountain streams and sway in the wind. The delicate blooms, like cherry blossoms, don't last long, as Basho's haiku reminds. The petals "rain down" into the mountain stream, and they, like us, are carried toward the rapids that we can only hear. The yellow petals will disappear under churning water and be carried out to sea; an image poetically descriptive but poignantly suggestive that offers a glimpse of the bittersweet nature of life. We cannot stop the petals from falling into the river anymore than we can stop the river from flowing over the rapids and down the mountain to join the ocean.

A time of *mono no aware*, our lives, like the fragile and fleeting kerria, sway precariously in the spring wind of our pandemic. In the weeks and months ahead, many will be touched by loss and the remembrance of someone's inner beauty: their kindness, sense of humor, generosity, contribution, or perhaps simply their struggle or failures, their unique "corner of light." Every Friday on the PBS Newshour four or five individuals who have died from COVID-19 are memorialized. Some die at over 90, others are in their 50s or 60s, a few are in their 20 and 30s, a father of five only 44. They come from all walks of life: a violist with the New York Metropolitan Opera; a perinatal nurse described as funny, humble and gracious; a football coach and mentor with "broad shoulders for carrying the worries of others"; a National Guardsman in a medical unit who died while preparing to help others. When we hear about real lives, human accomplishments, how people express themselves in our "fleeting world," we are struck by how utterly unique we all are, how every life is a one-of-a-kind, complex pattern, a gem reflecting light.

Around the time of kerria I went back to re-reading Sei Shonogan's *The Pillow Book*, an eleventh-century classic intended to be a travel book for our Japan adventure. Written in the Heian Period (roughly between 990 and 1002), Lady Sei writes about life at the Imperial court—then situated in Kyoto or Heian-kyo, the City of Peace and Tranquility, commonly called "the Capital." Her musings lent a bit of witty, light-hearted relief from the otherwise depressing daily news and death counts. Quite fond of making lists, she enjoyed the mundane, the comical and the serious. She also liked names: names of mountains, markets, peaks, plains and ponds; and made lists of them, perhaps relishing the way a word felt on her tongue or in her mouth, or what the place name evoked. On the funnier side, she listed, "Infuriating Things": hair in your ink stone; a dog that discovers a clandestine lover; or, "A man you've had to conceal in some unsatisfying hiding place, who then begins to snore." On the serious side, her lists included "Disquieting Things," "Moving Things," "Things That Prove Disillusioning."

In the Time of Kerria, I made a few lists of my own:

"Disgusting Things":
— a warehouse full of illegally traded pangolin scales;

"Disturbing Things":
— People dying without family present.

"Unforgivable Things":
— Medical staff with a shortage of PPE, in one of the "richest countries in the world";
— Workers without health care, in one of the "richest countries in the world";
— People living pay check to pay check, in one of the "richest countries in world."

"More Disturbing Things":
— Meat packing plants that rely on undocumented workers for cheap labor;
— Meat packing plants without adequate hygiene;
— Meat packers too afraid to call in sick;
— Meat packages;
— Meat.

In the Time of Kerria, and COVID, slaughterhouses and meat packing companies (both considered "essential") initially continued processing pigs, chickens and cows in the usual manner with workers standing shoulder to shoulder on fast moving conveyor belts. Their working conditions, perfect for coronavirus transmission, soon produced the inevitable result.

The average pig processing plant kills 1000 animals per hour. In the US, half a million pigs are killed for human consumption every day. If the animals cannot be "processed" rapidly and timely—for example, in a pandemic when slaughterhouses shut down to prevent virus spread—then a chain of events in the entire meat production line eventually forces farmers to euthanize their animals. By late spring, nearly 16,000 workers in the meat industry had become infected with COVID-19. Sixty-five would die. Plants closed. Farmers, forced to euthanize millions of their animals, either by shooting or gassing, agonized over their choices. Surprisingly, they did not find sending millions of animals to slaughterhouses in any way disturbing. In the farmer's mind, a euthanized animal had not "fulfilled its purpose" (food for meat eaters); this idea of "unfulfilled purpose" left famers feeling depressed and suicidal.

By the end of April, my kerria finally bloomed, but it produced very few yellow flowers. The long arching branches had more leaves than blooms. *Mono no aware*—kerria's lack of bloom production seemed to be saying, *I just wasn't up to blooming this year*. I didn't have the heart to cut any for ikebana. Instead, I made a mental note that one of the plants needed less sun, and the other needed better nutrition—the pine trees and aggressive native salal wanted to reclaim all my flower beds. Kerria was up for sacrifice. Should I let nature have its way? Should I surrender?

Nature wanted to do what it does; the virus was doing what viruses do; and humans do what humans do; after two months of lockdown seclusion, the end of April and beginning of May brought forth the "streaming" phenomena. Humans needed other humans, if not in person then virtually. With dharma centers closed and meditation retreats canceled, isolation from others—at first like a sigh of relief, a retreat—soon resurrected people's yearning for connection. Social gatherings, classes, discussion groups and meditations moved onto electronic devices. Resistant at first to a virtual life, I too soon joined the masses with an opportunity to study and meditate with two local Buddhist groups.

In our age of global pandemic and technology, everyone with a computer or a smartphone signed up for a Zoom account. Resisting technology, like resisting the virus, or the massive animal slaughter, or the mounting death tolls, were all equally futile. Nature, virus, humans, all doing what they do. Virtual gatherings soon became our norm.

By early May I'd joined the Olympia Zen Center's book study group: *The Essence of Zen* by Sekkei Harada Roshi. That same week, our island's Zen meditation group, a collection of women who had been meeting at Kandis' house or mine every Friday for the last eight years, formed our own Zoom group. We began our first meeting with a 25-minute meditation followed by a discussion of "The Great Awakening the Planet Needs," an interview of Joanna Macy by Melvin McLeod. The conversation between these two long-time Buddhists touched on the web of life, being present to suffering, and seeing our connection to other life forms. Joanna Macy recalled a quote by Thich Nhat Hanh, which I highlighted in yellow. When asked, "What [do] we most need to do for the sake of our world?" He'd answered, "to hear within ourselves the sounds of the earth crying."

I could hear that cry, the cry of a world out of balance, a world suffering daily losses of rain forests, elephants, tigers, ancient glaciers, polar bears, pangolins.... The earth had its own rhythm and order; the animals had their own rhythm and order. Humans seemed hell bent on disrupting rhythm and order. Encroaching into wild animal habitat, eating animals, had brought the coronavirus into human habitat. The rhythm and order had been disrupted. Should I let the salal have its way? Maybe kerria belonged on a different mountain, in another land, in its native land? Should plants, anymore than animals, be displaced, made to live in foreign homes? More questions than answers seemed to be the state of affairs. For now, two kerria plants lived in my yard on the mountain, on an island in their non-native land. All I could do is try to be a gracious hostess and offer them my hospitality. From kerria's healthier years, I savored an arrangement made with her previous bounty: gently arching branches as backdrop to pink parrot tulips.

Kerria with tulip

Chapter 5

Rhododendron-Azalea in the Time of COVID

we human beings
squirming about among
the flowers that bloom
Issa

April 22, 2020, marked the fiftieth anniversary of Earth Day. The worldwide death count jumped to over 200,000; and Jane Goodall, in an interview on the PBS Newshour, said, "We are all interconnected, and if we don't get that now, maybe we never will."

Will we get that? Will we wake up from whatever dream we're in that, pre-pandemic and still today allows 3 million children to starve to death every year without any government shut downs; that turns a blind eye to 70 million refugees without triggering a worldwide pandemic style mobilization? Will we come out of this global crisis awake to our interconnectedness and become a more compassionate world? I thought again of Sekkei Harada's words warning us that without cooperation we as a species wouldn't survive the twenty-first century. All the signs seemed evident that we foolish Homo sapiens might write ourselves out of world history.

A day like many others during "Stay Home, Stay Healthy," I went on a 3-mile walk along our mountain road: a circuit with small hills and twisty turns, old growth firs and a wetland pond with silver snags. Upon returning, I liked to check in with the plants in my garden to see who was up, who wasn't, and who was getting ready to bloom.

My Nancy Evans rhododendron had fat crimson buds ready to burst into golden yellow; and Bow Bells was showing the first sign of pink that would soon transform into clusters of bell-shaped blooms. *Ah, something positive about to emerge on this Earth Day in the time of COVID.*

Ramapo would bloom a little later and worked well for Saga School's Pond Scene; Mandarin Lights would be a good pick for heika, an informal style in a tall vase; and Polar Night bloomed even later; it had striking fan-shaped leaves perfect for modern styles.

By the end of our "Stay Home" order on May 4— which would be extended—I turned for a little relief to the many hybrids of our state flower, the coast rhododendron (*Rhododendron macrophyllum*). Selected by a group of women in 1892 to represent Washington at the Chicago World's Fair, rhododendrons, including azaleas which are in fact members of the Rhododendron genus, account for 1000 species and hundreds of hybrids. They, in their intense vibrant hues, promised to help fill the void left by canceled classes, canceled zazen, canceled trips, canceled everything.

The more imperiled realities of the sick, the unemployed, the worried, fearful and grieving continuously played in the background of my secluded life on the mountain, but the soft pink iconic symbol of impermanence: cherry blossoms, made way for the flower that symbolizes in Japan "remembering home": the Rhododendron azalea. Rhododendron, on the other hand, the non-azalea rhododendron, signifies "caution" and "danger" as the plant's leaves are highly toxic, but also indestructible—a quality it had every right to be known for although I hadn't found any such reference. Many times I've observed rhododendrons looking near death, their leaves curled and tortured under intense heat, drought or prolonged severe cold only to bounce back after favorable conditions returned. My rhodys, before the deer fence, endured having all their leaves completely consumed, but managed to leaf out again in April. Not even a week of sub-freezing weather with unseasonably deep snow curtailed their arrival in spring with green leaves and flower buds. Nothing, it seemed, could squelch rhododendron's force, or keep it from expressing its "corner of light."

In Japanese literature you don't find an abundance of poetic references to azaleas and rhododendrons, but since many azaleas grow wild in the mountains and produce beautiful pink and red trumpet-shaped flowers, a few discerning eyes would understandably take notice. In the *Tale of Genji*, written in the eleventh century, the author includes azalea in Prince Genji's special spring garden, the one he creates exclusively for the love of his life, Murasaki. In the *Manyoshu*, or *Collection of Ten Thousand Leaves*, an anthology of ancient tanka poetry, a mother thinks of her son as "handsome as azaleas": a more general reference to "youthful beauty" I suspect.

In modern Western times, azaleas and rhododendrons bring a zing of life to our cultivated gardens, especially in Washington State where they thrive. When we could view them again in our own parks, gardens and arboretums was anyone's guess; all public places were closed to prevent the spread of infection. Whenever these public places do reopen, will we pause from our fears and worries to appreciate them in the way they are sometimes characterized: "Everything is better with you!"

A week away from our "Stay Home" deadline, Boeing workers have been ordered back to work—some reluctantly, and some refusing, questioning their leader's judgment about safety. On the day declared "Stay Home, Stay Healthy," 70,000 Washingtonians worked at Boeing. But now, five weeks later, with half of all jets parked on tarmacs, who could possibly be ordering airplanes? One hundred and fifty of the 737 Max had already been canceled. In the days to come Boeing's woes would continue.

In similar news, more businesses reported either barely hanging on, folding or reinventing themselves. Some thought it imperative to get back to work; others thought it imperative to stay home a little longer. Some businesses shut down again when the virus reared up and created an outbreak storm. On the island, several businesses closed their doors for good, including several gift boutiques and our island's one and only florist shop and yoga studio.

In the meantime, Earth Day reminded us to honor our Great Mother, Gaia. Even in our time of uncertainty and global pandemic, "now" was always the time to revel in nature's beauty, variety, color and complexity: the continuous circle of priceless change. Honoring nature felt "essential," *was* essential. Had we already forgotten that pre-pandemic we were headed toward the cliff of climate change and mass extinction?

"Planting a Forest Could Help Prevent the Next Pandemic," says the Earth Day Network. Climate change disrupts breeding patterns. Deforestation brings humans closer to wild animals, closer to the diseases they carry and transmit to us through no fault of their own. Three out of four new infectious diseases come from animals.

Yet, left undisturbed, nature has the powerful potential to bring us humans in harmony with ourselves. Revisiting the purpose of our "flower temple trip," the word "celebration" came to mind, "appreciation," even "worship," "revere," and "venerate." Earth Day is a time to bow down to spring, earth's abundance and our relation to it.

Rhododendron with tulips

An email alert from the *Seattle Times* brought me back to the relative: "Boeing Pulls Out of Its $4.2 Billion Purchase of Embraer." Although another disaster for the company and our state's economy with more lost jobs, less airplanes might make the earth happy: that many more carbon dioxide producing machines won't be mucking up the air.

How to balance jobs with preserving the eco-system? How to shift away from fossil fuels, from technologies that pollute air and water, that produce climate change and world disaster? Important questions we were about to tackle before the novel coronavirus jumped to humans. Will this virus force us to change our habits? Or will we hop right back on the track leading over the cliff once the pandemic ends?

Another email, this one from Zen Mountain Monastery,

changed the tone, "In these times when so much is lost, practice remains...." Indeed, there's always "practice," as in "Zen within stillness, and Zen within movement," Sekkei Harada's two-part breakdown of our waking lives. He urges us to put our whole body and mind into our work; to put our full attention on whatever it is we are doing—whether formal meditation or housework, sitting on our cushion or sitting in front of our computer; be awake, aware, engaged. Be present!

On Earth Day, 2020, a glance at our Japan trip plans—in that long ago distant reverie of a dream life, when I created the document, "Proposed Itinerary for Japan"—had us viewing azaleas and rhododendrons at Mimurotoji: home of 20,000 azaleas and 1000 rhododendrons. Mimurotoji, in ancient times, was one among a string of temples to the east of Kyoto meant to shield the capital from evil spirits. Located in Uji—in *The Tale of Genji* considered a wild and desolate place—a wandering priest described it as a "lonely land, where the sound of water gave a feeling of washing the dust of anxiety." Today Mimurotoji is known for its vast azalea and rhododendron garden in spring, hydrangea in June, lotus in the heat of summer and maples in autumn. Temple No. 10 on the Kannon 33-Temple Pilgrimage circuit, Mimurotoji has been home to an ancient Kannon ever since an apparition appeared in the area. The statue, a Senju Kannon, or Thousand-armed Kannon, with an eye in each palm, not only sees all the suffering of the world, but metaphorically extends a hand to help. At this temple Thousand-armed Kannon is only revealed to the public once every 33 years—33 being symbolic of his/her manifestations as stated in the Lotus Sutra— but in 2020 the Buddha of Compassion would be needed 24/7.

Nyoiji, Temple No. 7 of the "Twenty-five Flower Temples of the Kansai," also enticed visitors with its spring azalea show. They advertised a newly renovated "flower and peace" garden that stands at the entrance to the grand pilgrimage site, an entire mountain covered in native Mitsuba azalea. Rev. Yuya Tomamatsu and his family care-take this temple located well off the beaten track on the Japan Sea. Like other abbots with "flower temples," he will, if asked, offer a dharma talk before touring the grounds. In today's world, I wondered what he'd say. When I went to my computer to send him an email, a pop up appeared to the side of my screen: Washington's total positive cases, 13,319; deaths, 738—up 104 since the previous week. Six months later, these numbers would look like a good day.

In other Washington COVID news, twenty-four correction officers and thirteen inmates have tested positive. More than 1000 inmates are in quarantine. A lawsuit seeks early release of at-risk Washington State prisoners in danger of contracting the virus. The two serial killers included in the group have raised public alarm. To the relief of family members of victims, and others, it was eventually struck down by a 5-4 ruling.

Contact tracing is being ramped up, Washington being the first state to use contact tracing back in January when we thought we had the first COVID-19 patient in the US (later evidence would put Santa Clara, CA, on the map as "first in US"). By mid-May, when rhododendrons will be at their peak, Governor Inslee wants 1500 trained contact tracers in full swing. His goal is to test 20,000 to 30,000 people a day. In April we had capacity to test 4000.

Three days after Earth Day, when I'd normally be preparing for two back-to-back ikebana classes, I sat at my dining room table looking out at the pale gray sky wondering what the day would bring. The rain had stopped, momentarily, but the wind, still blowing through the tops of tall firs, warned *not good conditions for a mountain walk*. I texted my sister Gwen who lived next door something to that effect, and we agreed to walk in late afternoon after creating some ikebana arrangements. The day before we had chosen maple branches with barely emerging leaves and the Bow Bell rhododendron for a heika arrangement. Most of the daffodils were hanging their heads, and although my Northern Gold forsythia still ablaze with sunbeam blooms had looked promising, it was "bloomed out" so to speak: on the back side of being used for ikebana which favors bud stage or barely open.

A phone bleep signaled a CNN news alert with the latest from the WHO: "no evidence people who have had coronavirus are immune from re-infection." This virus really would have the last say.

I scooped up an ant crawling across the table and put it outside; it was the fifth one that morning; then I pulled out a sheet of notes scribbled down from *The Essence of Zen* and read, "the main purpose of practice is to bring an end to the seeking mind and to live accepting your present circumstances." Hmm! Ants too? Viruses? Pandemics? I guess he really did mean "acceptance," as in "this is it," this is the experience of the moment, like it or not.

By the end of the Time of Rhododendron, as I watched the trumpet flowers of Polar Night transform from clusters of the deepest magenta into clusters of brown mush, I observed the leaving of this world in a new light. Plum and cherry blossoms flutter down from above like pink confetti at a child's birthday party. But rhododendron cling on and on until a heavy rain or a gloved hand separates the petals from the plant. The rhododendron's leaving had no grace or charm, but imparted a gift nonetheless: the nature of "clinging" or "attachment," sticky brown flower shafts that stuck to gloves, shoes and fingers. Rhododendron might be loved for their burst of bright color in the subdued skies of the Pacific Northwest, but they were not worshipped for their poetic way of transitioning.

Deep in the throws of a pandemic, on Earth Day—surely a time to ponder the human equation in the Gaia eco-system, a time to practice non-clinging—rhododendron showed me that hanging on to the way it was, to yesterday, to "normal," to what should have, or could have been was… well, a little ugly. Attachment felt "sticky," something you wanted to shake free of and be done with.

Chapter 6

Wisteria in the Time of COVID

all beings are flowers
blooming
in a flowering universe
Soen Nakagawa

"Splendid Things: Long, richly colored clusters of wisteria blossoms hanging from a pine tree" (Sei Shonogon, *The Pillow Book*).

In Japan, some varieties of wisteria (*fuji*) grow wild in the forests. They wrap themselves around trunks of trees and send blooms hanging down under limbs. In the Noh play *Fuji*, the ubiquitous "traveling monk" stops to admire one of these wisteria entwined around a pine tree. The scene reminds him of an old poem, and, depending which version you read, the poem either hails the pine and demeans the wisteria, or laments the monk's downfall. Neither poem pleases the spirit of the wisteria who transforms into a woman and appears before the monk. She criticizes him for reciting a poem lacking beauty and elegance; then remembers another ancient poem and recites, "Blooming by the lagoon of Tagonoura, the wisteria blossoms are reflected in the water, coloring the waves purple."

The monk appears humbled, and the woman, admitting that she is the wisteria spirit says, "Think of me as the spirit of ethereal flowers, existing between dreaming and awakening." That night she appears to the monk in his dreams to tell him she "was enlightened by the Dharma of the Buddha and became a bodhisattva of flowers."

In *The Lotus* Sutra, the most revered Buddhist teaching in Japan, Regarder of the Cries of the World Bodhisattva (aka

Kannon/Avalokiteshvara) transforms into whatever humans need for liberation. *Perhaps a wisteria?* The chorus intones, "It is the flower blooming in an enlightened heart. Even the seaweed and grasses attain Buddhahood." Then the wisteria spirit reminds the monk that "transience in this world agrees with the law of nature. In particular, the wisteria flowers fall almost as soon as they bloom."

At this point in a Noh drama a slow dance accompanied by Japanese flute and drums assists the audience in entering into the unseen world of the spiritual essence of flowers and trees. The lead actor and flautist track their breaths during a performance in order to stay synchronized; and in an ideal performance the audience too would harmonize their breath with the performers; thus entering into the unseen energy of the unseen world.

The breath, that all important bodily function that means life or death, resonates in myriad ways. We breathe in life's oxygen and exhale carbon dioxide, while plants "breathe in" carbon dioxide and "exhale" oxygen. The unseen rhythms keep the world of nature and sentient beings in balance.

In pre-pandemic time (December, 2019), as excitement mounted for our "flower temple pilgrimage," Kandis emailed a link to a famous wisteria temple in Aichi prefecture; it boasted 60 wisteria varieties in purple, lavender, red and white. Bloom times indicated mid-April to May. I penciled it in on the itinerary ahead of azalea and rhododendron viewing at Mimorotoji in Uji.

Three centuries earlier, while on pilgrimage to famous and historical places, the haiku poet Basho, weary and in poor health, wrote:

exhausted
seeking an inn:
wisteria flowers

In *Zen Wave*, Aitken Roshi commented that, "At the very point of despair, Basho encounters the rich lavender wisteria flowers," implying that their essence, at least temporarily, mirrored the poet's melancholy and simultaneously lifted his spirit.

Wisteria with rose
Original container by Mika McCann

In the Time of Wisteria, New York funeral homes became overwhelmed with the deceased, and stories emerged of corpses in body bags stacked inside refrigerated trucks awaiting retrieval and transport. Retail stores struggling to reopen in regions with lower positive cases had to combat customers who refused to wear masks.

After our governor extended "Stay Home, Stay Healthy," I became obsessed with wisteria—having one and growing one. Good, deep soil for growing plants as vigorous and demanding as wisteria did not exist on the mountain. Mostly we had mossy boulders, and areas around house, septic and propane tank where excavators had removed them. I'd had a "landscape guy" put in good soil around the house, but the rest of it.... I'd struggled over the years beefing up the clayish construction soil with compost and chicken manure, but with disappointing results. I did *not* have a good place to plant a wisteria: no soil, nor a support sturdy enough for its energetic vines. What I did have were seven oak wine barrels cut in half. They worked for clematis, peony, lupine, iris, chrysanthemum and even a Korean witch hazel. Why not wisteria? The guy at the big box store on the mainland said they had plenty of wine barrels. Usually they were sold out.

The plan got hatched to go off island to get as many wine barrels as would fit in my car, then head to the big nursery in the valley for a prize wisteria. The wisteria would grow in the wine barrel and trail over the shed. Our county had moved into Phase II reopening with some travel restrictions, but growing my own wisteria suddenly felt "essential"; after all, islanders were going to the mainland to buy toilet paper at Costco.

I thought of the wisteria vine that hangs over the courtyard at our local co-op, and the one draped around the porch of Kandis' house; the vine that twists around a pole at the now closed pizza place; and the one anchored to a giant trellis at my sister's suburban condo complex; then there was the spectacular pink variety that grew over the pond at the Seattle Japanese Garden—that one truly held the presence of *kami*. I thought of all the places where I'd admired wisteria; it was high time I had one of my own. I too sought respite in the long lavender racemes. Wisteria... definitely "essential."

With mask, sanitizer, lunch, and water bottle, all packed, I caught the 8:55 a.m. ferry, which would get me to the mainland by 10:00. I had until 2:00 p.m. before panic set in to get in line for the 3:05 return.

The ferry, on time and not very crowded for a day in May, got me to the big box store within my timeline. Upon arrival, and with no clerks in sight, I proceeded with my mission to score half-wine barrels. I went up and down every aisle in the outdoor garden center three times—no half-wine barrels, only whole ones. *What would I do with that?* The guy on the phone *apparently* had not grasped my desire and obsession.

The next best thing was fake wine barrels made with flimsy wood and thin metal straps. I couldn't bear going home with nothing after coming all this way; in a pandemic! Three "fake" barrels made it onto my cart.

I wasn't the only one feeling that gardening was "essential." The check-out line trailed past the table of blooming perennials, gallon shrubs, racks of garden hoses, ceramic pots, and ended way in the back by wheelbarrows. All of us obsessed plant lovers, masked and six feet apart, pushed our carts little by little to the front. With an eye on my watch, others turned an eye on the line and gave up. *Maybe one geranium and a marigold weren't essential?*

Finally in front of the cashier after 20 minutes, I made one last attempt to acquire "real" wine barrels, which resulted in holding up the line until yard help could be found. I imagined all the people behind me grimacing behind their masks. In the end, no half-wine barrels could be found. I apologized to the couple standing six feet back and left slightly embarrassed.

By the time I got to the nursery, time edged toward the "Cinderella hour" when all islanders feel the fear of leaving the ball in time to catch their coach back to the island. If I missed the 3:05, the next ferry wouldn't leave until 7:10; and occasionally, quite occasionally these days, the ferries broke down and runs were two hours late or canceled.

The aisle with wisteria, way down the last aisle of the nursery, had several beautiful burlapped vines in bud stage. I favored the Japanese variety Black Dragon; the name and abundance of blooms spoke enchantment, spoke of wisteria spirits, Noh plays, poetry and ancient Japan. *But could I grow it in a pot?*

"What?" asked the masked clerk, trying to hear my question through three layers of flannel sheet material.

"Can I grow Black Dragon wisteria in a pot?" I repeated.

She shook her head. "It wouldn't like it."

Wouldn't like it? Could I do that to a wisteria? Keep it confined in a fake wine barrel? My fantasy world crashed under the weight of attachment. I had to let go of the wisteria dream for now, and opt out of imprisoning a vigorous vine for my own gratification.

Disappointed but not defeated, I headed to the peony table. Another peony shopper hovered in the area. Together we did a six-foot social distancing dance around the peony table. One plant in particular caught my eye: an expensive Itoh named Sequestered Sunshine with five fat buds. Peony Shopper saw it too. Impulsively I grabbed the yellow peony and loaded it onto my cart; the attachment demon had returned.

Arriving at check-out, and another line, one glance at my watch said, don't dally. The clerk wrote up my slip; I paid the cashier; and off I scurried with my cart. Once at the car, I reached into the side pocket of my purse where I always keep my keys. Nothing—the pocket was empty. I *never* misplace my keys. They have a designated pocket on the outside of my purse and that is where they *always* go.

Not believing that my car keys *really* weren't there, like an automaton with a power glitch I checked three times; went through my entire purse, twice; checked each of my jacket pockets, twice. Eye glasses, now fogged over from breathing heavily into three layers of protective face covering, impaired my vision and orientation simultaneously. *Try not to panic. Be present. Take a breath.* But living on an island complicates the most minor problems. If I couldn't find my keys, I'd have to call a locksmith... I guess. But locksmiths open locks so you can get your keys out of the ignition. My keys were not in the ignition. They were missing.

I needed a Subaru Outback car key. The extra one remained safely back home, on the island, on the mountain, worlds away.

No keys in purse. No keys in pockets. No keys on the ground. No keys. My house keys and mail box keys were on the same ring as my car keys. *Did my sister have a key to my house? I thought so....*

Look in every pocket, again. Search through every compartment. Go back to check-out. Ask if there's a "lost and found." Go inside the office. "Did you find a set of car keys?"

The clerk held up a black remote and jangled the keys, her grin only partly concealed behind a mask. "Are these yours?"

My last stop on my big day of "essential-non-essential travel" took me to Starbuck's drive-thru—the only part open in those days. I *needed* a matcha latte, maybe even a "forbidden" chocolate croissant. The line, like all lines during those early days, trailed around the building and into an overflow parking lot. It wasn't moving. All itineraries, necessities, cravings, attachments took second place when you have a ferry to catch. In the back of my mind I heard a famous Roshi saying, "Don't cling to anything," as I pulled out of line and headed to the terminal.

By the time I got home, around 5:30 p.m., my imagined "fun" day doing "normal" things left me exhausted, anxious and cranky. Peace of mind, present moment Zen practice? All gone. Now I was supposed to stay quarantined for 14 days, even though I'd been careful with mask, sanitizer, and hand washing, and I'd been mostly outdoors. Still, every day for at least a week, every little twinge in my chest, sensation in my throat, slight drop of blood pressure, a gurgle in my stomach... all COVID symptoms. I'd return to feeling normal until the next imagined warning sign; then another wave of anxiety would wash over me. Ah, the self-clinging mind. How we cherished this ever so impermanent physical body. Was this to be our norm now? "The fight between the True Self and the ego-self," as Sekkei

Harada says. Fear and anxiety, uncertainty and unknowing; all the time. Practice intensified.

Each day infections rose, deaths continued. Everyone said the only hope was a vaccine, and toward that end world leaders from Japan, Canada, Australia and Europe had pledged millions of dollars. But the US had not joined. Was this the face of "America First"? Everyone's very breath, speech, and touch was capable of either connecting us with our fellow humans or inadvertently infecting them with a microscopic virus. We are the individual petals of a wisteria pedicel, connected as one pendulous raceme, hanging together, swaying in the winds of uncertainty. How will we live during our brief time of blooming? Will we exude a pleasant scent?

Wisteria, cultivated in Japan for well over 1000 years, can live to be 100. Because of its longevity it is considered a symbol of wisdom. The long hanging clusters resemble the act of bowing, or kneeling, and the spiral pattern of the wisteria vine in Buddhist thought symbolizes the "unfolding of consciousness reaching out to the divine."

For three, maybe four weeks, the wisteria will express its "corner of light," but all during the time of wisteria, the chain of tragic events brought on by consumers not consuming reached far and wide. In Bangladesh, where all our cheap clothes are manufactured, retail giants in the West stopped submitting orders.

I thought of Sei's lists and penned this one:

"Heartbreaking Things":
— Women garment workers losing their only source of livelihood;
— Women with no unemployment benefits or stimulus rescue packages;
— Women who could not feed themselves or their children;
— Women and children.

Upon waking each morning, Gwen remarked that it took mere seconds to shift into the reality of the pandemic: death, unemployment, collapsing economies… a mere few seconds for despair to filter back in.

Wisteria mirrored our hanging heads, reflected our melancholy; the lavender hues, most admired at twilight, colored our nation and world in a state of mourning. *After a weary journey—wisteria!* Expressing our feelings and relieving our feelings at the same time.

Chapter 7

Peony in the Time of COVID

by itself
the head is bowing...
peony!
Issa

The Friday before Memorial Day weekend, in the Time of Peony, something flu-like: chills, body aches, a slight fever; settled into my body. COVID-19? Without a sore throat, cough or high fever, and not having traveled, been exposed to anyone positive or been anywhere that would indicate COVID infection, I dismissed the possibility. The fever disappeared the following day along with the chills; within 48 hours the body aches had ceased. Only a little tiredness lingered. I called it pandemic fatigue, but perhaps it was something else. Psychic overload? The body anticipating the negatively charged wave about to engulf the country? Who can say!

Far removed from the world where sirens wail into the night, I found solace in my lemon-yellow peony, Sequestered Sunshine, blooming ahead of the others. Even in the rain it stayed true to its name, creating an aura of potential optimism, of something bright to come... someday. But wasn't the future a dream story yet to manifest, a bud not yet opened? Better to stay in the present moment: the flower opening; and contemplate the medicinal potential of peony, both physically and spiritually.

Eighth-century Buddhist monks brought peony, the "King of Flowers," to Japan from China for the root, flower and seeds, all tonics for inflammation, arthritis, muscle cramps, lupus, spasms and fever. And if you live in Japan, you can enjoy peony's magic in spring *and* winter—the *kan-botan* or *fuyu-botan*, meaning "winter peony" is cultivated in temperature-controlled settings that force them into bloom from December to February. Each plant, protected from snow by a little straw house that looks like a conical hat, also gets a straw mat to protect the foliage from rain splashing up from the ground. Peonies are this cherished.

Peony with ginger and flax leaves

Not feeling up to my daily walk, I mustered the energy to stake the tall white peony I'd planted in an oak wine barrel two summers back. Having thrown away all my plant tags the last time "this isn't it" crazy mind had me making plans to move off the island, the white peony was now "the white peony": very fragrant with single petals and a yellow center. I also had a dark red peony, a pink peony, magenta peony and salmon. The white peony had finally produced a profusion of buds, and promised to be heavy with abundance in about a week. Others I'd planted had mixed reviews. The striking dark red peony I'd planted in the propane tank area had one bud. A handful of ants dined on its sweet nectar. The pink one, planted among trees and shrubs, had now become too shaded and required more sun to bloom. I made a note to move it in the fall, even though peonies don't like being moved; it was for its own good. The one that last summer looked like it was dying, rallied back with a plethora of salmon buds. The one starting to be overwhelmed by a forsythia bush had only produced one magenta bud, but lots of striking foliage.

Success in growing peonies remained a mystery. Not understanding the formula for creating consistently fully blooming plants, the regimen of composting, fertilizing, and making sure the eyes didn't get covered, continued each season. As a child in North Dakota, I remember riding past an abandoned farmhouse with my mother, and seeing a peony in full bloom. Nobody lived at the farmhouse. No one tended the peony: watered, fertilized or composted it; but it bloomed anyway. Mother couldn't resist. One day she stopped the car and helped herself to a bouquet. I've heard others say how easy they are to grow. *Just plant them in the ground. They bloom every year.* But here on the mountain, with poor soil, strong winds and native plants like salal, wild rose, mahonia, wild strawberry and trailing blackberry hell bent on reclaiming their territory, peonies had a hard battle. Where did humans have their place in this eco-system? My presence had upset the lives of so many. The ants, for one, had their colonies disrupted and destroyed. The many native plants had been excavated, bull-dozed, trampled, pulled out by the root, and hacked off with sharp tools. Trees had been cut down, or limbed. Squirrel homes had no doubt been lost, bird nests unsettled, and hundreds, perhaps thousands of micro-colonies also dislocated or disordered. Hadn't everybody—other life forms I mean—survived just fine before us humans came onto the scene? The pandemic itself had arisen out of transgressions into the kingdom of wild animals. The displacement of the natural world went unnoticed in the city where it was easy to forget that a meadow or a grove of ancient cedars had been replaced by a parking lot or a skyscraper. But here we are, still hacking our way through forests and jungles, still disrupting the natural order of things, still trying to dominate nature, and each other.

In the Time of Peony: Memorial Day weekend; our nation would reach the milestone of 100,000 American deaths from COVID-19, but we would also reach another apex: the tipping point where racial injustice could no longer be tolerated.

On Memorial Day, May 25, 2020, an unarmed black man named George Floyd bought a pack of cigarettes at a convenience store in Minneapolis. The clerk detected a counterfeit $20 and called 911. Within 20 minutes of the police arriving on the scene, Mr. Floyd would be lying on the sidewalk unconscious. For over 9 minutes the white police officer held his knee to Mr. Floyd's neck. "I Can't Breathe" were his last words before he lost consciousness. "I Can't Breathe" would soon be heard in all corridors of our society. African-Americans had struggled against racial injustice and oppression since the days their ancestors had been forcibly brought to the shores of the "New World" aboard slave ships. After 400 years, our country's sin reared up to be reckoned with.

The front page of *The New York Times Sunday Edition* listed the names of those who had died from COVID-19: a "memorial wall"; but it could have been 100,000 African-Americans who had died from lynchings and police brutality, from all the white knees on black necks.

Demonstrations, mostly peaceful; and rioting, mostly not peaceful, erupted in every major city in the US, and even abroad. People cried for racial justice everywhere. "I Can't Breathe" became the plea of the oppressed, the sick and the world of nature. It seemed that the whole planet felt on the verge of suffocation.

Hacked by an alleged Nigerian crime ring, Washington State's Employment Security Department lost hundreds of millions of dollars at a time when thousands of unemployed needed to pay their rent. The anxiety of the unemployed, another cause for impaired breathing, sent another unsettling ripple across the landscape of our state and nation.

Whether to mask or not to mask, open businesses or close businesses, took on political overtones as Americans with guns marched on state capitals demanding their constitutional freedoms and liberties. Others, counting on their neighbors to do the right thing and prevent the spread of the coronavirus, looked on wondering about *their* freedoms and liberties.

The Governor of North Dakota pleaded with his constituents to "dial up empathy" and remember "North Dakota kind; North Dakota smart; North Dakota understanding." He laid forth a path of reason and sanity, a path we could take, if we wanted. Was there a will for that? Did we want to be kind, smart and understanding?

On the morning of Memorial Day, 2020, not yet tuned into the day's news, I sat at my dining room table reading a dharma book. When I looked up there was Sequestered Sunshine. It looked happy. After a week of dry weather, we'd had a good rain. The whole garden looked happy.

In the greater world, before the death of George Floyd, not all the news was grim. Japan lifted its State of Emergency, and some normalcy returned to a few countries. Peonies would continue to bloom while Washington State, once the epicenter, transitioned into opening more businesses. Infectious numbers leveled out, and for a time, the virus felt slightly under control. Once again, we fell for the illusion of "safety." Either way, the virus didn't care.

Secluded on a mountain on an island, far removed from urban demonstrations, protests, freeway closures and other forms of people rightfully reaching their breaking point, I turned again for a little relief to the language of flowers and a stack of haiku books on my desk. Hoping to find the perfect short poem on peonies, I picked up R.H. Blyth's *Haiku, Vol. 3* and found ten pages devoted to the elegant flower.

Issa, Shiki, and many others, all had their say about peonies. One by Buson offered the possibility of transcendence:

about to bloom
and exhale a rainbow—
the peony

We needed rainbows these days, rainbows of the wishing kind. And what did I wish for? Perhaps it was the same wish all over the world: that humans could find happiness on earth; that all women and men would be treated equal; that this pandemic would end; that the virus that was killing hundreds of thousands (nearly 350,000 worldwide on Memorial Day, 2020) would disappear as quickly as it had arrived; that the unemployed would be employed again; that the sick would heal; that opposing ideologies would come together for the good of all; that people would matter more than stock; that we could all take off our masks; that we could put our hand sanitizer in the back of the cupboard where we'd found it; that we could hug our family and friends without fear; that we could go out to eat; that life would return to the life that we once thought to be normal but that now looked like a dream we once had; in fact *was* a dream we once had.

My white peonies, getting ready to bloom, getting ready to exhale a rainbow, looked hesitant, looked as though they didn't believe in rainbows. "I Can't Breathe" kept ringing throughout the world, a man calling out to his mother in his final moments before death—a death that one coroner claimed to be asphyxiation and another said heart attack. But neither was the truth. George Floyd died because he had not been allowed to have his "corner of light," his chance to be the person he wanted to be.

"I Can't Breathe," began to reveal the true 2020 prophecy of attaining "clear sight": millions of Americans couldn't "breathe" under the tyranny of racism, poverty, unemployment, low wage jobs, racial injustice, inequality, and white supremacy agendas. People couldn't breathe under all the decades of neglect, being overlooked, humiliated, oppressed, and murdered.

We were a country that suddenly couldn't breathe, and it took the dying words of yet another persecuted black man for Americans, and the world, to see that as a country, a nation, we were suffocating from lack of empathy, compassion, generosity and loving-kindness. We were not "kind, smart or understanding." We had not reckoned with our history. We had not told the truth and been reconciled.

By the first week of June, Sequestered Sunshine's petals had scattered to the wind, becoming food for insects and billions of micro-organisms lying hidden in soil, bark and moss. Protests continued, the coronavirus continued, death counts continued... On the morning of June 5 our island Zen group discussed an article titled "Meditating with Emotions," by Pema Chodron. "[B]uddha nature includes everything," says Pema. "It's the calm, and the disturbed, and the roiled up, and the still; it's the bitter and the sweet, the comfortable and the uncomfortable." That same day, in another state, Nobuko Ohgi, a Saga Goryu practitioner and teacher, a former *sensei,* who passed the torch of Japanese flower art to many over the years, died from a lung disease.

As I awaited the blossoming of later peonies, especially my mysterious white one, sunny days, even when the sun came out, had a tinge of overcast, and rainbows were nowhere to be seen. This too was Buddha nature.

Chapter 8

Iris in the Time of COVID

purple cloud —
isn't it the same color
as the iris?
Chiyo-ni

Purple cloud... Cremation smoke? The celestial vehicle that transports bodhisattvas between human lands and Pure Lands? The color "in a field somewhere" that would incur the wrath of God if you failed to notice? On the Kannon pilgrimage of Western Japan, many a temple site designated "sacred" came about through legends of a "purple cloud" appearing in the sky before a significant event.

Iris, like plum, conjures a promise of hope, but on June 12, 2020, the time when iris overlaps with peonies that overlap with rhododendrons and hydrangea and dozens of intensely bright spring/summer annuals, a time when nature bursts with fertility and abundance, another unarmed black man, Rayshard Brooks, father of four, was shot and killed by a white police officer. Hope for racial justice slipped away, again. The world watched yet another horrific taking of human life via video camera. Atlanta erupted with violent push back. The fast-food franchise where Mr. Brooks had fallen asleep in his car, and fallen in death at the hands of an officer's three bullets, got torched. Bright flames of rage burned into the night while the $10,000 reward offered to anyone identifying the arsonist as yet unclaimed. All the while, COVID-19 spread too like flames across the continent along with protests over the killing of George Floyd.

In another Noh play about the enlightenment of flowers, *Kakitsubata,* or water iris—just like wisteria and numerous others—begins with a monk on pilgrimage. He stops to admire the water irises growing at the edge of a pond when a young woman appears and asks him why he lingers so. He says that he's admiring the beautiful irises; and she tells him that this place is the subject of a famous love poem from the *Tale of Ise* written by Narihira about Princess Takako. She then invites him to stay the night in her humble lodgings, and he accepts. Before the monk settles in, the woman changes into a spectacular kimono, and an equally stunning headdress—garment and headdress said to be that of Narihira and his lover. She begins to sing and dance, thus revealing that she is the spirit of the water iris who has received enlightenment through the powerful words of Narihira's poem and the merit of Buddha's law. The chorus sings "It is a tale without beginning, a tale without end, a tale about the love of a man... iris reminded him of his wife, who was left behind in Kyoto... only the color is left."

At the end of the woman's dance, she sings of the iris' heart of enlightenment, that even grasses and trees can attain enlightenment. At dawn she disappears.

Siberian iris

In Japan, iris symbolizes the purification of evil energies and forces. With its trigonal, or three-fold symmetry, the open iris resembles a simple mandala, a conduit for higher vibrational light. With its many positive and celestial suggestions, it is not surprising that the iris motif has not only decorated many Japanese kimono as a protective talisman for the wearer, but has also been the subject of numerous paintings and poems throughout the centuries.

Every culture has powerful symbolic imagery conveying the language of the mysterious iris. On the other side of the world, in ancient Greece, the word "iris" means "rainbow," the name of the Greek Goddess said to swirl through the universe on rainbows that link our earthly realm with the heavenly. When planted on grave sites, the goddess Iris leads the deceased beyond the suffering of earthly existence. I didn't know if there was such a place, but in the Time of Iris, it was comforting to think that a realm existed where human suffering might be vanquished, where viruses didn't exist, where guns didn't exist.

In China the petals of purple iris are likened to butterfly wings fluttering in the breeze. On other occasions they are hung over doorways to dispel evil spirits.

Iris viewing had not been on our Japan trip itinerary for the obvious reason that they do not bloom in April, but if ever the opportunity presents to travel the Flower Temple Pilgrimage in June, Temple #11, Eitakuji, in the mountainous region of Hyogo prefecture, with its Japanese Iris Garden (right next to the Flower Carpet Garden of "one hundred million pink phlox"), will most definitely be on the list.

Ponds of white, yellow, purple and variegated irises: three million, in six hundred and fifty varieties; surround a watermill and running stream at Eitakuji. Zig-zag wooden bridges that cross wet areas and waterways in the *feng shui* and Japanese/Chinese style are meant to confound evil forces (according to legend, harmful spirits can only walk straight lines). In Zen philosophy, the zig-zag bridge also ensures that the observer stays centered, present and undistracted. One stray thought might send the flower struck observer tumbling head first into the deep.

In late spring, Iris descends for a short time and paints the garden with her rainbow colors, hues that soothe us weary humans. The spiritual allure of the iris bloom offered potential respite, but in our time of COVID and killings, the cultural metaphors pointed to yet another part of the world—the sword-like leaves are said to mimic the sorrows that pierced the heart of Mary as she witnessed her son Jesus dying on the cross.

Unlike plum or cherry blossoms that flutter poetically and dreamily through the air once they've reached the end of their life, the iris bloom curls up and folds into itself as if withdrawing its light from the world. By the middle of June, the iris' manner of leaving mirrored my own feelings. Racial justice protests continued and COVID infections continued unabated as everyone struggled to reopen businesses, to return to "normal life"—the desire understandable, but with the coronavirus unleashed, "normalcy" remained elusive. It was a "tale without end," a "tale about the love of a man…," or a woman, or a child, or a father, mother, sister, brother… all those "left behind" mourning loss. Even our nation, in deep mourning for victims of COVID and police shootings, for a way of life or livelihood, hovered over our world as another kind of cloud.

On the mountain, my bearded irises bloomed first, followed by Siberian, Dutch and Japanese. In truth, I only had one Japanese iris due to its preference for wet or semi-wet soil— not in great abundance on a mountain with dry summers. None of the other irises seemed to mind the lack of rainfall. With nearly 300 species and 50,000 registered varieties, an iris species and cultural metaphor exists for everyone's taste, temperament and climate.

Toward the end of June, the last iris to bloom in my garden would be the pale yellow Dutch irises followed by — theoretically — my one Japanese white iris. The rest of my irises: the dark purple Siberians, the light purple bearded, and the lavender with striped foliage; had already passed on and left. The garden filled with little iris petal fetuses all curled into themselves. The white Japanese iris, nearly buried under a spreading Solomon's seal and denied adequate light, never bloomed at all.

Chapter 9

Hydrangea in the Time of COVID

the spirit, the truth
of silent prayer —
just the moon on the road
Kikusha-ni

In the Time of Hydrangea, the US reached its highest per day increase in coronavirus cases: 50,000 (but winter was yet to come). The virus had been spreading out of control in half of the US where social distancing, wearing masks and avoiding large gatherings had been ignored. In Texas, ICUs had reached capacity. Still the president held indoor rallies and refused to wear a mask, or to encourage others to wear masks. He flaunted the three Cs: Closed, Crowded, & Close.

Sekkei Harada says, "[I]t is necessary to free yourself from thinking that things must be this way or that way. This too is the meaning of the first teaching, 'all things are impermanent.'" World events and the direction of our country consistently challenged adopting this view. Could I really be an impartial witness? Yes, events would change. The pandemic would end. One day we would have a different president with a different orientation, but suspending judgment when so much was at stake... well, felt impossible. It would mean sitting with sadness, grief, fear, anxiety — all the emotions I wanted to avoid. If things went a certain way — my way, went my reasoning — I wouldn't have to feel sorrow at all this avoidable suffering.

Hydrangea, or *ajisai,* means Gathering of Blues in Japanese. Native to Japan, hydrangea carries a feeling of melancholy as it blooms during the rainy season. Some say the rain enhances the color, but others prefer to see the predominately blue flowers against a sunny sky.

In modern times, hydrangea comes not only in blue, but pink, rose, white, and shades of lavender, all dependent on the soil's Ph. *Nanahenge,* or seven transformations, is ascribed to hydrangea for this reason as the petals can change from light blue, to darker blue, to lavender and purple depending on the acidity or alkalinity of the soil. This changeability also marks it as one who has a capricious heart; therefore, further enhancing its already melancholy character.

In the language of flowers, hydrangea not only conveys a feeling of sadness, but, due to the tight flower clusters, also denotes family bonds and endearing love. Because of its many evocative qualities, hydrangea appeared in Japanese poetry as early as the Nara Period (710–794) and remains a favorite flower in Japan even today. Hydrangea festivals abound, and like cherry blossoms, people travel to famous hydrangea gardens and temple grounds to celebrate the mystical qualities of the flowers enhanced further by the foggy humid rains of the rainy season.

During my short tenure in Japan, and about two weeks before moving back to the States, my English students took me to the vast forested complex of Sanzenin Temple in Ohara, a region near Kyoto famous for hillsides filled with thousands of both common and rare hydrangea. The outing commemorated my leaving, a time filled with emotion for all of us. True to the Ohara region's reputation, a light fog hung over the mountain that day, creating the gauzy image favored by poets. Two photos I've preserved for twenty-seven years capture our day on the mountain. One photo shows a much younger me standing on a vermillion bridge between three of my students. I know that behind us and all around us, and on both ends of the bridge, are mountain slopes filled with blue hydrangea, but it's hazy and I can't see the flowers in the photo. I know the flowers exist because the other photo shows me crouched in front of a hedge of lavender blue hydrangea blooms. I look happy. My students look happy. We are reveling in nature's mysterious aura.

Thoughts of mystical blue hydrangea compelled me to stop at my favorite valley nursery on the return leg of an "essential" trip to Seattle. I relished the opportunity to assess nature's goods after an intense week dodging closed freeways and police clashes with demonstrators. A blue lace cap hydrangea, a light pink hydrangea, a struggling miniature hydrangea and one that hadn't bloomed (my mystery hydrangea), had found a home in my garden, but I *required* yet another one to fill one of the fake wine barrels purchased on my last trip to the mainland. The perfect spot with just the right amount of shade had already been prepared.

Once at the nursery I headed straight for the hydrangea green house; the many varieties of pink, white, mauve, blue, purple and even green gave me pause. Was I confident that it had to be blue? Yes, a blue *Hydrangea macrophylla* Bailmer one in the "Endless Summer" collection, a Japanese native. "The less you prune, the more it blooms!" proclaimed the tag on the only two left. I chose one in a five-gallon pot, bigger and more expensive than my usual plant purchases, but one that matched my "blue" mood. Seattle, my former home for over 25 years, had erupted with daily outrage over police brutality and racial discrimination. The collective angst of so many traumatized citizens lingered in the back of mind. During one of the freeway closures, as demonstrators blocked traffic to bring attention to the killing of George Floyd and other African-Americans, a driver deliberately plowed into the crowd. A 24-year-old woman named Summer Taylor was killed; and another young person was seriously injured. Tragedies like these—beginning to feel common place—heightened everyone's grief, fear and anxiety. What would happen next? Nobody knew. Our "practice" became staying present to uncertainty, bearing witness to suffering, and participating in "the Great Turning," a phrase first introduced by Craig Shindler and Gary Lapid in 1985, but since taken up by Joanna Macy to describe a shift away from world conflict and environmental destruction toward a higher level of consciousness, a planetary awakening. Were we "turning" in the right direction? It often didn't look or feel that way. And I suppose one could ask, who gets to determine which way is the right way? I calmed myself knowing that my little view was limited; the bigger picture eluded me. Like the photo from that day in Ohara on the bridge, I couldn't see the hydrangeas stretching up the mountain slope but I knew they were there, all around us.

Masked and sanitized I made my purchase and headed for the ferry. Going off-island to the mainland always carried greater risk of exposure to the virus, and a recent news bite played in the back of my mind: *COVID-19 strikes those with type A blood disproportionately.* I am type A positive. This new fear, along with all others these days, rose and fell like a wave. I took the ups and downs to the only place I could—my meditation cushion.

Our Zen group's recent discussion article by Pema Chodron advised us to "smile in the face of fear." Fear, that nebulous apparition hanging around the back of the closet, the one with an evil smirk on its face, now had a foe. I smirked back and intoned a childhood taunt, "You can't scare me." None of us were going to survive our life. We carry on despite our fears, order our groceries, pick them up curbside, fetch mail, check for messages, talk with our siblings, see our friends via Zoom, make non-essential trips off island, avoid freeway closures, cheer the protestors, and carry on. Over 65, previous heart condition, type A blood; I had my blue hydrangea for solace. That would have to be enough. Or at least I wanted it to be, and it did help. Like all the other seasonal blooms, hydrangea conjured spiritual essence, a perfect state of peace and purity. At least for awhile, until the next onslaught coming from the relative world caught me unaware, and, in the vocabulary of Thich Nhat Hanh, made me forget that my little "wave" of self (self with a small "s") is part of a "vast ocean," that deep well of eternal essence we try to name, and cannot.

Every day many opportunities arose to disconnect from the "ocean" of True Self. On the evening of July 3, a cold day after a week of intermittent showers, a rather large "wave" of anger came ashore. The president made an Independence Day speech at Mount Rushmore against the backdrop of all those white presidents chiseled into the Lakota Sioux's sacred mountains.

Dogen says, "If the least like or dislike arises, the mind is lost in confusion." With all due respect Dogen, as an American I couldn't remember a time when I felt so demoralized, embarrassed, and heartbroken. Amid conspiracy theory rantings, the president neglected to address the main elephant in the room: the pandemic. Numbers in the US had been skyrocketing like the jet planes and fireworks bursting above his head on Independence Day.

Yet there's this idea in Buddhism, born out of the opposite feelings that emerge in the Time of Hydrangea: the rainy season in Japan; that we can choose to view blue and pink and white hydrangea flowers with an unhappy mind or a happy mind; it's all in our perception, and the choices we make. Nothing is fixed; hydrangea in the rain is neither happy nor sad, good nor bad, only hydrangea blooming in the rain.

In the "Wisdom Teachings" column of the *Saga Magazine,* the author suggests that the hydrangea serves as a cue, reminding us that we always have a choice to perceive the good or the bad, to turn a negative into a positive. The hydrangea itself is not a fixed color, but changeable, fluid. It does not proclaim "this" or "that," but a "rainbow" effect: all inclusive. The "Wisdom Teachings" further suggest that to experience nature is to expand our own Buddha nature, our human potential. Trees and flowers help us "develop our own inner light."

I sought that light in the Time of Hydrangea, and at all other times, but more and more in our country's response to the pandemic and to racial injustice, I failed to find peace and found more grief. The grieving felt continuous and it was during this time that I heard the news about Sekkei Harada Roshi. Although I didn't know him personally, after reading and re-reading his words in *The Essence of Zen*, I knew that his light would be missed in the world. At 93 in the Time of Hydrangea, and in the middle of our country's surging infections, he left this world. Maybe he had seen enough for one life.

The "Memoriam" for Harada Roshi came into my email box from the Olympia Zen Center; it described this venerable monk as "a generous man," someone who could get angry but whose anger "dissipated quickly." "He could be joyful, and when he laughed, it was complete." "Roshi was a mountain of the Way... completely present... clear, fair, kind and strict." "[I]t was his job to point the direction for those who were seeking [the Way]."

The Way wasn't always clear, but like the changeable hydrangea, a period of grief could change into a moment of joy into a moment of boredom, anxiety, contentedness, and back to grief in the course of 24 hours. In the spirit of the nun Kikusha-ni's haiku it was best to keep one's eyes on the road where the moon kept lighting the way. Or an eye on the garden where the blue hydrangea settled into its container and continued to bloom; it offered inspiration for a new ikebana arrangement: a blue coronet with a dark pink Seaside Serenade (a sapphire with a ruby) nestled in a black matte *suiban* within the curve of an aged apple branch from a friend's 100-year-old orchard. Like all other flowers, they wouldn't last long, but much longer than plum or cherry blossoms; and the plant itself with its blue clusters *did* look better in the rain—multi-faceted, jewel-like, enhanced by cloudy skies and rain drops. In keeping with its name, Endless Summer, it would continue to bloom into fall, always reminding me that I had a choice: was the glass half full or half empty.

Hydrangea blossoms with apple branch
Original container by Paddy McNeely

Chapter 10

Lotus in the Time of COVID

a white lotus —
the monk decides
to cut it!
Buson

In *Haiku Mind,* by Patricia Donegan, the mystery of why the monk cuts the lotus holds the potential for a variety of karmic repercussions: "Many causes and conditions must coemerge for something to happen." To cut a flower as magnificent as a lotus implies a motivation shrouded in mystery. Was it a pure motivation, or one with possible peril? We couldn't know.

In the Time of Lotus, researchers at the University of Washington Medical Center found an antibody that could stop COVID-19. In the realm of the pandemic, this action had the promise of "hope." That's all we could say for sure. In the realm of racial justice, Portland saw its seventieth day of unstoppable protests against police brutality and racial inequality since the death of George Floyd. Would it move us toward "kinder, smarter, understanding"? More equitable action? Would more compassionate conditions result? As in cutting the lotus, perhaps the most important question to be asked and answered: What is your intention?

Lotus
Photo courtesy of Bruce Hamana

We humans have the potential to be beautiful flowers emerging from the "mud" of our lives—this is the symbol of the lotus. Buddha Shakyamuni, and all other Buddhas are represented in this way. Our "mud" is all that we grapple with: the obsessions, attachments, fears, worries, angers, hatreds, injustices... The lotus shows us that we can rise out of this "darkness" a glorious bloom. We can feel the encouragement of our potential emerging. This is the purity of our original spirit, our True Self, or our "face before our parents were born" as some say in Zen. The lotus rises up from the bottom of a muddy pond, but is not sullied. We can cultivate our lotus heart, and come up from the dirt and grime unstained. The lotus is human potential, awakening. The lotus, or *hasu* in Japanese because its seed pod resembles a honeycomb, was said to be the flower from Buddha Shakyamuni's famous wordless sermon, the "Flower Sermon." Buddha held up a white lotus and transmitted the wisdom of "suchness" to his disciple Mahakasyapa. This disciple acknowledged the transmission with a smile; and thus, it is said that Zen was born at that moment.

The lotus most identified with Buddhist iconography is *Nelumbo nucifera*, native to most Asian countries. But unknown to me until the time of this writing, we have an American lotus, *Nelumbo lutea*, with white to pale yellow blossoms; it grows east of the Rockies and south to Florida. The tuberous rhizomes and seeds, once an important food source for Native Americans, are mostly grown now for their decorative seed pods. Knowing about the American lotus gave me a sense of optimism. Perhaps we Americans could also rise out of the mud into a brighter, clearer world.

In the Pacific Northwest we don't have lotus, only water lilies—both aquatic plants but not in the same family. Water lilies, on the other hand, grow as a perennial in our mountain's pond, and in many wild and cultivated ponds in the region. The only chance of growing lotus might be in a large water garden, but probably not. Lotus likes hot, humid weather; something in short supply in the Northwest.

Even though I cannot grow lotus, or visit any nearby places with a lotus pond, or have it available to use in ikebana, it would be sacrilegious to write about Japan, Buddhism, and the language of flowers and not include lotus.

The ancient Japanese calendar—Season #32, "The First Lotus Blossoms,"—describes how lotus buds begin to emerge from the bottom of the muddy pond in the middle of the night (around 2 a.m.); then they slowly rise up and unfurl. By dawn they are fully opened. By early afternoon they have already closed. The lotus repeats this quiet ritual for three days. On the fourth day their petals begin to fall. In ikebana language the leaves are also significant: the rolled-up leaf represents yin (the female principle of the universe associated with earth); the wide open leaf represents yang (the male principle of the universe associated with heaven); and the half open leaf represents the harmony of the two: heaven and earth, body and spirit, working together.

One weekend in August, during my residence in Kobe, I tried to reach Kyoto early enough to witness a lotus opening; but, of course, it was never early enough. The story goes that the lotus makes a popping sound when it opens; some say the sound of enlightenment, but I've never heard it. The "sound" might be poetic imagination, or simply a "feeling" of sound. The lotus, a magical looking flower, is capable of evoking mythical lore; indeed, lotus flowers were said to spring up from the ground wherever Buddha walked.

Sound or no sound, I would need all the wisdom of the lotus metaphor to get through the summer of 2020. The US, my beloved homeland, continued to be the epicenter of the pandemic with the most infections and most deaths worldwide. By the middle of August, we had over 5.5 million infections and 170,000 deaths. Yes, scientists had a lead on antibodies, and worked furiously toward finding a vaccine, but everyone else it seemed worked furiously toward defying scientists. Schools opened, and then closed. In the first two weeks of classes infections surfaced and spread. The Coronavirus Aid, Relief, and Economic Security (CARES) Act that offered additional unemployment benefits to millions of Americans, ended and was not renewed. Congress met, discussed, wrangled and failed to institute another aid package to help the 30 million unemployed. Food Banks in my state began to stock emergency supplies. Everyone anticipated a tidal wave of evictions and homelessness. The virus spread out of control, and yet Sturgis, South Dakota, would host its annual motorcycle rally that traditionally attracted between 500,000 and 700,000 people. In 2020, in a pandemic, 460,000 motorcycle enthusiasts showed up and threw caution to the wind.

By the middle of August, the natural world: flowers, trees, even weeds; looked exhausted, their life force spent. Summer annuals struggled to bloom through heat and drought. Trees began to shed brown crispy leaves; more than a few fluttered down during my morning walks. Americans too showed signs of exhaustion as we faced the fact that many schools would not be reopening, nor would restaurants, bars and gyms be returning to anything "normal" for a long time.

Yet with everyone yammering about social distancing, mask wearing, and hand sanitizing, we as a nation did not seem capable of putting a lid on this virus. In the Time of Lotus, we routinely registered 60,000 new infections every day. New Zealand, on the other hand, celebrated 100 straight days of no infections. Japan, registered 52,460 infections and 1073 deaths — lower numbers than my home state that crept toward 70,000 infections and 1800 deaths. Even Italy, once the epicenter of the pandemic, had "flattened their curve." How did we, one of the richest, most technologically advanced countries in the world get to this dismal juncture? It seemed we suffered from an acute case of either outright denial or cognitive dissonance: a state where you know a behavior is harmful but you do it anyway (i.e., you don't wear a mask, don't social distance, don't sanitize) denying the facts.

When we entered Season #38, "First Autumn," the Japanese almanac described a feeling of sadness found in the singing of the cicada. Like the lotus, here in the Pacific Northwest we didn't have cicadas either, but the memory of them on a hot and humid August day near the edge of the rice fields in Hyogo Prefecture still lingered as a vivid memory. In Japan, when the cicadas sing their mournful song, it is also the season for lighting lanterns and candles, and making prayers for the dead. O-bon celebrates the deceased, a time when ancestral spirits are said to return to earth for a kind of family reunion.

When I first arrived in Japan in August of 1991, our group of teachers and friends were treated to a weekend in the countryside where we danced the traditional O-bon dance, as is the custom. At that time, even without knowing much about Japan or its traditions, a melancholy feeling permeated the slow rhythmical movements performed in a circle after dark; the dance brought with it a feeling of the transience of life, the end of a season, a time of year that one could feel the incoming days of darkness and winter. Life energy, having been spent to bring flower and food into our world, now redirected itself toward rest and renewal; it would re-emerge in spring.

A friend remarked that everyone had been complaining of exhaustion. Another friend came down with something akin to pneumonia, but tested negative for COVID. She slept a lot, and took long afternoon naps—not her norm. A weariness settled in.

The news media too seemed tired of the same story: virus spreading, deaths mounting, not enough testing or tracing, many still not wearing masks or keeping socially distanced. All year, as the pandemic raged, we as a country also grappled with upcoming presidential elections. Joe Biden, a white 78-year-old Democrat had been chosen to run against the president, a white 74-year-old Republican. We awaited Mr. Biden's vice-presidential pick, and in the Time of Lotus he made his decision. She would be the first African-Asian-American woman to ever be on the presidential ticket. Her nomination, unique in the history of our male-dominated nation, gave us all a break from the normal news. Kamala Harris promised to deliver us from an all white, all male line-up, but more than that she marked perhaps a turning point for our nation toward racial and gender equality, and perhaps even more. Coincidentally, "kamala" in ancient Sanskrit means "lotus flower."

True to fashion, for the next few weeks, depending on which news outlet you trusted, we would hear that Ms. Harris was either an intelligent, capable, experienced candidate or a hollow puppet of questionable birth. This too was all so tiring. The only respite came from that quintessential Buddhist metaphor: the holy lotus, and the Zen teachings that reminded us that all things, both positive and negative, don't last; we are all interconnected and of the same essence; and that Nirvana exists in the here and now. Without this source of Buddhist refuge: a life raft in the middle of our American ocean of insanity; I might have drowned a long time ago. Lotus, although not in my literal world, provided ballast in my spiritual one and shone like an ancient lantern lit on a hot August night; I could see it rising up from the bottom and welcoming the dawn.

Perhaps the monk cut the lotus so Buddha could hold it up, so we could see reality as it is, the forever now; that image, especially in the Time of Lotus and all times, was most definitely "essential."

Chapter 11

Cosmos in the Time of COVID

flowers scattering—
the water we thirst for
far off in the mist
Issa

As we entered into the Time of Cosmos, wild flowers, the ones not getting the benefit of human watering systems, had all packed it up for the season. The deep violet thistles admired during a morning walk, had transformed into fluffy white down. Daisies turned from perfect white petals with cheerful yellow centers into rather stinky waves of shriveled up brown. Foxgloves, bent heavy with seed pods resembling large rosary beads, readied to release next year's crop. Mullein, once stately with rabbit soft gray-green leaves and bright yellow flowers had withered into erect cathedral spires that remarkably would withstand the wind, rain and snow of winter. COVID too had apparently transformed, from a deadly "L" strain virus from China, to a deadly "G" strain virus from Europe. Although the jury was still out on this "two strain" theory.

My cosmos, or *kosumosu,* seedlings, having gotten off to a bad start from inadequate light, struggled all through spring and summer. Bright Lights, the rare yellow-orange variety, produced one small plant with crooked stems and tiny flowers. It fizzled out by August. Daydream and Versailles Red produced a few solid but sparse plants—nothing like I imagined. A week before the end of September, I held out hope for one plant that had grown lush and tall but had yet to bloom. Then a few days after it formed buds, around the time of autumn equinox "when night and day have equal say," says the almanac, and the US

98

reached 200,000 deaths from COVID, a rain and wind storm pelted the promising cosmos into submission. One of Ryokan's flower poems came to mind:

> My garden flowers
> I planted and nursed myself
> With genuine love,
> I must learn to resign them
> To the pleasure of the wind

The grand master that promised a plethora of rich red or pink blooms cracked at the base and fell over defeated. Only Sonata, the white variety—white being symbolic of either purity or death—produced the strongest plants with enormous and prolific flowers. Not even our unseasonal September storm beat it down; and as long as I kept watering and deadheading, white cosmos, like the death toll, marched on undaunted.

The miracle of a seed cannot be overstated. The "apparitional" voice in Clark Strand's *The Way of the Rose* so eloquently states, "A seed is like a small hammer that cracks the silence of the soil with its voice." So many seeds, both literal and figurative, had been planted in 2020. Some had sprouted and bloomed; others waited for new leaders, wise voices, the presidential elections, and the time that followed. Had we been careful in our sowing? Had our nation?

Back in 2018, when we visited the "cosmos temple" of Hannya-ji, the first "flower temple" of the Kansai Twenty-five, I had imagined our visit to be the beginning of a story on flower temples that I would tell... someday. But cosmos conjured other memories, one's from childhood and teenage years when I observed my mother's garden. Every year she sowed a swath of cosmos, and every year I wondered why she found those simple little flowers so delightful. Was it the ease in growing? One of the few things that gave her a feeling of success and purpose? Or maybe, like me, over time Mom discovered cosmos' poetic charm, the delight of simple things, uncomplicated and unentangled from politics and pandemics. Beginnings... Does the story of cosmos begin with my mother in my childhood? At Hannya-ji in Nara? On March 13, 2020, when I planted nine packets of cosmos seeds that had waited for sun, soil and water ever since the last trip to Japan? I contemplated transformations—a child's view, teenager, mature adult. Cosmos had not changed one bit over the years; it remained steady, predictable, reliable; but I had changed. My view had begun to shift slowly and imperceptibly to just noticing. Suspend judgment and opinion and what do you have? The world unfolding in myriad ways, energies changing, forms shifting... Even the cosmos temple in Japan had transformed from a once thriving monastery with 1000 monks in residence into a small neighborhood temple in the back streets of Nara where modern day flower temple pilgrims traveled in autumn to make offerings to the bodhisattva of compassion.

Hannya means *Prajna* in Sanskrit: the word for wisdom, as in the "Wisdom Beyond Wisdom" of the Heart Sutra, an ancient teaching studied, copied, recited, and cherished in Buddhist centers throughout the world. The essence of the Heart Sutra states that there is no beginning or end, no birth or death, that life is an interconnected, ever-changing phenomenon with no inherent or fixed nature or permanence. One thing flows into another, and another; "things" beget other "things" in a continuous cycle called impermanence. Seeds do not independently arise. Before becoming a cosmos seed, there was a cosmos flower pollinated by a bee or butterfly. The plant that produced the flower, and later the seed, required soil, sun and rain to grow and produce next year's seed. The seed could not arise independent of all the other conditions any more than we could independently arise without the earth's great elements. So too pandemics. One action begot another and another. A decision to mask or not mask, to socially distance or not, all led to consequences — causes and effects.

The previous year (2019), in the Time of Cosmos, the same time we finalized our Japan reservations: flight, inn, airport shuttle; a scientific article posted on a Swiss non-profit publishing site called MDPI stated, "This is the first report on the viral diversity of pangolins, expanding our understanding of the virome in endangered species, and providing insight into the overall diversity of viruses that may be capable of directly or indirectly crossing over into other mammals."

Like most people, I didn't routinely read scientific journals, nor did I have any knowledge of pangolins (the most trafficked mammal in the world), or virome (assemblages of viruses), or zoonosis (a virus transmitted from animal to human), but here we were, one year later with staggering statistics that corroborated the theories, studies and warnings of viral transmission. One person in Wuhan, China, became infected with a rare virus, possibly via a pangolin, and within 12 months our country went from its first positive case on January 21, to its first death on February 26, to 7.5 million positive cases, and 210,000 deaths. By October 1 in the Time of Cosmos, the world would come in at 35 million infections and 1 million deaths, and yet the previous year, 2019, when pilgrims were making the annual trek to Hannya-ji to revel in the poetic nature of cosmos, the US government began to quietly phase out funding for research on dangerous animal viruses that could infect humans.

In the Global Health section of *The New York Times*, this article caught my attention: "Scientists Were Hunting for the Next Ebola. Now the US Has Cut Their Funding." The program, called PREDICT, set up and funded to find viruses that could jump from animals to humans, might have prevented COVID-19. The month before, in September, the World Health Organization and the World Bank stated in an article by the

Center for Infectious Disease Research and Policy (CIDRAP) that "the world isn't prepared to respond to a pandemic and that proactive efforts are needed to detect and control potential outbreaks." As far as I could tell, none of the research, opinions and professional work of these scientists had been taken seriously by our government or other world leaders.

Had it only been two years since that sunny day in Nara, taking photos of magenta, pink, yellow, orange and white cosmos: 150,000 blooms in 30 varieties; all of their little nodding heads encircling statues of Kannon, the Boddhisattva of Compassion? Although so beloved in Japan it is known as *akisakura*, or autumn cherry blossom, cosmos is native to Mexico, and takes its name from the Greek *kosmos*, meaning harmony or ordered universe. Cosmos has eight evenly spaced petals arranged in perfect symmetrical order around a bright yellow center: a world replicated in delicate petals encircling a perfect yellow universe. The number eight itself carried Buddhist symbolism: the eight-fold path that leads to liberation; the eight auspicious symbols of sacred offerings; December 8, Buddha's enlightenment day; and, "the eight basic concepts that serve to fuel our fear," says Thich Nhat Hanh, "and the teachings given to counteract these notions—the eight no's—no birth, no death, no coming, no going, not the same, not different, no being, no non-being." Cosmos, with its perfectly arranged eight petals, inadvertently pointed to the truth of emptiness, that nothing exists independently. We humans cannot be separated from the plants we eat, the animals we slaughter, the water we drink. Sun, rain, soil, plant and animal matter become these bodies the same as flowers. The elements generate cycles of seasons, transforming substance into substance without end. We are all made of the same elements; we breathe the same air, move in the same space, take in and transmit microscopic particles: viruses. We are interconnected in unseen ways, and express our

interconnection through talking, laughing, hugging, kissing—
now with literally deadly consequences. To kiss a baby or a
bride, hug a friend or the bereaved, to laugh, sing or simply
speak, exposed us all to a possible death sentence. Yet the bright
pinks and crimsons of nodding cosmos light the late summer
garden undaunted by our human conundrum.

Cosmos with miscanthus and peony leaves

Brought to Japan by Italian artists, cosmos immediately became
popular. The long stems that sway in the wind appealed to the
Japanese sense of the poetic, to entrusting oneself to the "winds
of impermanence": a feeling of the ever-present reality of nothing
fixed or static, but always changing, moving, transforming. We
too, as a nation, could not avoid these ominous breezes.

Not always a pilgrimage site where flower lovers revel in

brightly colored cosmos intertwined among bodhisattva statues, Hannya-ji, as reported in the *Tale of the Heike,* was the site of a conflict between two warring clans. The temple burned to the ground around 1180. In retaliation, the chief commander during the time of the fires, was nailed to a torii gate at Hannya-ji for having ordered the fire from that spot. Consequences! Cause and effect! There is no escaping it. Actions eventually catch up with you.

Once known for its kerria, or mountain rose, Hannya-ji saw its first cosmos about fifty years ago when a small patch in a corner of the temple grounds began to flourish; it gradually took over. The delicate flower, thought to evoke loving feelings, easily adapted to the Japanese climate. Cosmos, in the right conditions, re-seed themselves, not only at this temple, but in fallow fields, along railroad tracks and other wild places. Acres of cosmos can be seen bobbing in breezes around the "praying hands" traditional cottages still found in the Japanese countryside.

After Hannya-ji I'd been inspired to grow bushels of cosmos; thus, all the seed packets; but again in 2020 I planned to be gone the majority of spring and wouldn't be around to water and nurture them. The seeds would have to sit on my desk through another season.

But then, like a spring breeze, life quietly changed direction, requiring me to explore the multi-layered symbolism and poetic feeling of "flower temples" virtually, like an ancient armchair traveler conjuring imagined worlds. Another autumn and here I was, on a mountain, on an island, in my own garden, finding solace in flowers in the Time of Cosmos, in the Time of COVID. Thick into the pandemic with no end in sight, thick into racial injustice with no end in sight, thick into killings and gun violence with no end in sight, and then literally, thick into smoke from fires raging out of control with no end in sight; all these crises took us beyond the pandemic and racial reckoning to the ravages of climate change. It had struck again. The US West Coast, shrouded in an oppressive blanket of wildfire smoke, smoke from burned trees, burned homes, animals, pets and pet owners, pushed air quality into the "red zone": unhealthy; with warnings to close windows and stay inside. The smoke lingered for days and days, filling outdoor spaces with the stench of burning and dangerous particulate matter that health experts warned "could settle in your lungs." Indoor spaces too filled with smoke; it sucked oxygen out of the air. Breathing became strained and suffocating, our life force smothered by something invisible. Once again, anxious fearful emotions filtered into the corners of our lives, and the words, "unprecedented" and "apocalyptic" became all too common adjectives.

Every month since the Time of Plum, a new crisis arose in the world and here at home. In the Time of Cosmos, fires in Brazil ravaged the Pantanal, the world's largest tropical wetlands; and the fires in California, Oregon and Washington were the worst on record; in the Atlantic 23 named hurricanes had already emerged; and the Thwaites Glacier in Antarctica showed signs of rapid melt. Ironically, with the threat of earth being inundated with walls of ice and flood waters, the UN Secretary General said at the 2020 Climate Change Roundtable that, "the world has a high fever and is burning up."

We had already forgotten that, before the pandemic, millions had rallied worldwide to bring attention to our changing climate and the march toward the Sixth Extinction. I thought of the three sharks visual in Joanna Macy's "Pandemic as Practice": a worldwide sharing of our collective grief. The little Great White Shark: "COVID-19," chased after a lone diver in a big blue ocean; the middling Great White Shark: "Economic Crisis," chased after the little shark chasing the diver; and lastly, the giant Great White Shark: "Climate Change," opened its mouth wide and threatened to swallow everyone, echoing Roshi's words "as long as there is no mutual support among people…

we will become extinct in the twenty-first century."

The water we thirst for! Had we found it? *Flowers scattering...* as summer headed into autumn into winter. Cosmos too would scatter, one petal at a time, curling in like crumpling cosmic whirligigs. One by one the petals shriveled and fell leaving the perfect universe: the yellow center; then it too shriveled, but not before producing a mound of seeds that the wind, in its wisdom, would scatter far and wide. If the seeds fell on fertile soil, they would arise again the following spring bringing another season of "little Buddhas." Flower Temple priests echoed the words of Dogen Zenji when he said, "Flowers teach us how to smile." In the pilgrimage literature, the abbots confidently asserted, "Flowers are like little Buddhas." Surely, we could agree that we needed more Buddhas, more "awakened ones" in our suffering world. Perhaps cosmos, with its nodding heads of perfectly ordered petals, was here to remind us.

Chapter 12

Chrysanthemum in the Time of COVID

white chrysanthemum's
unchanged shadow—
print of the moon
Chiyo-ni

In the Time of Chrysanthemum an assortment of shocks, ironies and tragedies played out against the background of the magical transformation of summer into autumn. Gaps left by falling deciduous leaves began to fill with a tangle of political fact and fiction, reality and fantasy, as crisis after crisis unfolded.

First, a wave of the virus swept through the West Wing of the White House, and beyond, infecting dozens of people in the president's circle, including the president, his wife, their young son, a former governor, a general, an admiral, a senior advisor, two military aides, the press secretary, two reporters, two housekeeping staff, a campaign manager, a Republican chairwoman, three senators, and a college president. The president, hospitalized at Walter Reed Medical Center, and given a dizzying array of medications: the steroid Dexamethasone, the experimental drug Remdesivir, Regeneron's monoclonal antibody (still in clinical trials but approved by the FDA), Famotidine (still in clinical trials), Melatonin, aspirin, zinc and vitamin D; briefly left on day two (still contagious) for a spin around the hospital with Secret Service personnel. Dozens of flag waving supporters had gathered outside. The job of a Secret Service agent is to "comply" and "protect," but not "give one's life" in service. Already over 130 agents had contracted COVID-19.

Released on day three (still contagious) the president said, "Now I'm better, maybe I'm immune, I don't know." He told the nation not to let the virus dominate their lives while 9000 Americans died that week from COVID-19; and nobody, not the CDC or virus experts, knew how long immunity would last after contracting the disease.

Infection numbers in the nation, and the world, kept rising with dire predictions of a second wave in the upcoming months. Disease experts warned of the troubling winter ahead. The pandemic presented plenty for all of us to worry about, but equally concerning were circulating letters and speculations that a political coup d'état was in the making for our upcoming election day. We should be prepared, the information said, to stage a massive strike to save our democracy.

In years past, my memory of autumn remained a time of creativity and fresh energy, a time to take a bucolic scenic drive into the Cascade Mountains for fall color viewing (so Norman Rockwell sounding these days), or, in lucky years, a time to visit Japan and revel in the stunning maple leaves adorning hillsides and ancient temple grounds. In comparison to 2020, those days felt dreamlike and disturbingly carefree. With "Staying Home" dictating most of my activities, I spent the latter days of October and the first three days of November trying to stay centered and sane in the whirlwind of politics and social upheaval. Practicing ikebana with the few cosmos that made it to maturity, and the late blooming hydrangeas, steadied my mood. All the while I kept an eye on the tub of chrysanthemums growing in one of the half-wine barrels. My life could be a simple life, a hermit's life, one focused on meditation, writing, flower arranging... except for one thing: the bombardment of national news with its endless stories of human suffering that infiltrated my otherwise peaceful sequestered world. I couldn't tune it out or ignore it. I couldn't stop it.

We had just finished with the time of fire and smoke, a time that required an N95 mask when venturing outside. I'd strapped mine on to gather flowers, while checking in on the progress of the chrysanthemum buds getting ready to open wide into our strange new world. Their strength and resilience inspired me. They were survivors. Years ago, when my sister and I bought our first set of half-wine barrels, we planted chrysanthemums (*kiku*) in every color. All of them made it through the first winter. The next autumn big bushy chrysanthemums filled three barrels. But over time, through drought, snow and subfreezing winds, one by one, the mauve, white and rust-orange succumbed to one thing or another. Now in 2020, only the golden yellow chrysanthemum—the same color Confucius admired in 500 BC—remained. In the days ahead, as world events escalated out of control, the yellow chrysanthemum moved me with its ability to endure, and brought me back to the country that it symbolized, Japan. The monarchy itself, referred to as the Chrysanthemum Throne, carries the flower as its imperial crest; the wild chrysanthemum that grows on an island in the middle of Osawa Pond at Daikakuji Temple so inspired Emperor Saga that 1200 years later the Saga School of Ikebana still tells the story.

Daisy chrysanthemum with Japanese anemone

Temples in Japan normally hosted chrysanthemum displays in late autumn. Some hobbyists created bonsai, others chrysanthemum dolls, or simply potted plants featuring gorgeous king and spider chrysanthemums. Annually, Daikakuji gardeners train and prune chrysanthemums into the heaven, earth and human configuration of seika arrangements. Tall, six-foot plants adorn exterior temple courtyards festooned with fall's scattering scarlet leaves.

On the home front, a memory of last year's autumn brought a momentary smile when I recalled running into one of my ikebana students in town. Standing on the street corner surrounded by crispy colorful fall leaves, the subject of "raking" versus "leaf blowing" came into the conversation. Joni made a sweeping motion, and, with a satisfied grin on her face, proclaimed her fantasy job: sweeping a temple compound. Her arms moved back and forth, and for a moment she disappeared into a dreamworld.

On the Kannon pilgrimage that my sister and I completed in 2015, we remembered two types of temples: leaf blowing temples and broom sweeping temples. The mere mention of "leaf blowers," made Joni shake her head disapprovingly. "No, no, no," she said, before I could finish the sentence. At the mere words "broom sweeping" her smile returned.

I recounted the day we visited one of the small neighborhood temples on the Kannon pilgrimage in rural Japan. Upon entering the front gate, we heard our favorite sound: bamboo broom bristles moving across stones. A blissful smile spread across Joni's face while she resumed the gesture of sweeping, sweeping, sweeping. "I'd like to visit that temple some day," she said.

There's a story often told in Buddhist circles about a monk who couldn't memorize any sutras, or debate any philosophy. He couldn't keep up with the other disciples and scholarly types. So the Master gave him the job of sweeping the temple, and over time, concentrating as he did on the back and forth motion of the broom, and imagining sweeping away delusions and obstacles, he became enlightened. The story mirrored Sekkei Harada's words about meditation in movement, about "an effort to be each thing, each activity, each moment."

The women sweepers of Anaoji, dressed in simple cotton dresses with print aprons and head scarves, expressed the beauty contained in humble acts: nothing flashy, nothing overly complex, just a woman, or a Joni, sweeping a real or imaginary temple. How could we get to that state? How could we, in the Time of Chrysanthemum, with so much turmoil swirling around us, be sweepers of the temple: a simple job, humble, necessary, physical, rhythmical and enlightening. How could we as a people sweep away our many delusions?

As a nation we grappled with our COVID numbers and shook our heads at the lack of a cohesive plan to control the virus. For some, our one hope became the elections on November 3, when we had a chance to replace a leader and an administration that had downplayed the coronavirus, lied about it, implied it was a hoax, and mocked scientific experts' advice on how to control it. Even this hope was fraught with anxiety when the president planted the seed of "ballot fraud" into the minds of the American public if he should lose, and suggested potential violence when, during a national televised presidential debate, he called upon a white supremacist group to "stand back, and stand by," refusing, when challenged, to condemn that ideology. Later in the month, one of those groups plotted to kidnap and put on trial Governor Gretchen Whitmer of Michigan. Early on in the pandemic, Governor Whitmer had instituted tough measures to control the virus. Apparently, some of her constituents didn't like her directives, nor, apparently, did the president when he'd tweeted, "Liberate Michigan!" The FBI arrested 13 men and charged them with "conspiring to commit kidnapping and providing material support to terrorist activities." The "13" had an arsenal of firearms, projectile launchers, zip ties, Tasers and explosives, all part of a plan to start a civil war.

Kidnapping plots! Civil war! Terrorist activities! Nothing surprised me these days. Yet I worried that I, along with the nation, might be growing numb to the daily onslaught of twitter feed propaganda, lies, false claims, divisiveness, bullying and conspiracy theories. It was all so tiresome, so mentally, physically and spiritually exhausting.

As the pandemic continued unabated, my aspiration to live a life as simple as "sweeper of the temple," played out against the dramatic dreamworld of domestic terrorist plots, rising infections, COVID deaths, social uprisings, unprecedented climate disasters, potential coups, and general world instability. The sharks were hungry, relentless; and then the buds of the yellow chrysanthemum began to open. Little daisy-like flowers filled the entire barrel like a big yellow Afro. Leaves of forsythia and burning bush began to turn color; peony leaves transformed into various shades of orange and wine red. In Japan, maples would soon turn scarlet, and float down, one by one, onto temple pathways where the *print of the moon* kept leading us along through the darkness, where the whoosh of bamboo brooms echoed along the pathways.

This autumn, the white chrysanthemum—in Japan, the flower of choice for caskets and tombstones—would honor the many dead in this "fleeting world," and more particularly in the USA, where the white chrysanthemum would cast the longest shadow. In Japan, on the other hand, the country we feared traveling to back in February, back in the Time of Plum, when we still reveled in mass gatherings to celebrate spring, COVID infections and deaths remained lower than our state alone. The USA, still the epicenter, registered higher totals every day, even though the CDC kept warning of "a whole lot of hurt" to come this winter if we didn't get the virus under control.

As we entered November, and Daylight Saving Time in the Pacific Northwest, autumn took a drastic shift toward winter. A few nights dipped below freezing and wiped out any remaining flowers: dahlias, the last of the cosmos, and late blooming hydrangea. Even my barrel-full of golden chrysanthemums turned toward brown. On the mountain, we had mostly conifer trees—no big leaved maples or Japanese maples, no stone courtyards or pathways to rake. In the first few days leading up to the elections, after the weather returned to sunny and mild, I practiced contentment by cleaning up perennial beds. Cutting rather than sweeping replaced the meditative rhythm as I methodically hacked down moldy and rotting leaves of iris, peony and crocosmia. The forsythia and burning bush had also turned the corner with more gold and red leaves on the ground than on the branches. My fall ikebana materials gradually disappeared. The hard, yet rewarding work of cleaning up the flower beds offset and dissipated the disturbing news of COVID numbers rising and the upcoming elections. Once all the garden flowers disappeared, I brought home armloads of king chrysanthemums from the off-island supermarket. For several days I arranged large yellow, burgundy and rust blooms with crabapple, spirea, fir, and the last of the forsythia branches. Chrysanthemums, although loved nearly equally with roses, survive twice or thrice as long. They keep blooming, blooming, blooming. The king and spider mums open like a cluster of long thin fingers, their collection of petals or "quills" supported on a cup-like bract. Sometimes you think the chrysanthemum flower will stay fresh forever. Weeks and weeks go by and still they hang on. But much like our health care workers who have carried on professionally in ICU wards for ten long months, the petals eventually show signs of slackening, as they get ready to fall. Fatigue was setting in. Burnout. Doctors and nurses only appeared as though they could go on forever. Underneath the cluster of quills, a process of letting-go had begun. Total exhaustion from months of unrelenting admissions and COVID deaths had taken its toll. One touch of the long lush quills and they collapsed all at once, sending still supple petals onto the floor or into your hand. By the Time of Chrysanthemum 1500 health care professionals in the US had died of COVID-19.

The day before elections, all the daisy chrysanthemums, like their larger sisters, had started to fall. Eventually, only the yellow disk would remain until it too would turn brown along with the pungent serrated leaves both edible and prized in ikebana.

On November 3, 2020, the day of our elections, the US reported 9.5 million infections, and 232,000 deaths. That same day, in the Southern Hemisphere, Australia reported no new infections. That's right! None. Zero.

Having cast my mail-in ballot early (Washington State transitioned to the mail-in ballot option fifteen years ago), I went to bed hoping to wake up to a nation with a new direction and the promise of a less foreboding shadow, one made shorter through wisdom and compassion. Little did anyone know that another crisis was about to bloom. In the US, 2020 wasn't over by a long shot.

Chapter 13

Camellia in the Time of COVID

the camellia—
it fell into the darkness
of the old well
Buson

Camellia, or *tsubaki*, blooms in the cold no matter what the political weather, no matter what the COVID count; it is the quintessential winter flower, and not only produces beautiful blooms but, depending on the cultivar, is grown for dye, oil, medicine, furniture and tea—the latter used in the Way of Tea, a meditative ceremony of refined hospitality conveying harmony, respect, purity and tranquility.

As our nation awaited final results of the presidential election, early camellias, the *C. sasanquas,* started blooming in the northern hemisphere. *C. japonicas* would follow, with various cultivars blooming well into spring. We would need these small wonders of nature to get us through *this* winter.

Flowering camellias, versus tea camellias (*Camellia sinensis*), are especially prized in the Japanese tea ceremony where a bud with perhaps an autumn branch is placed in a simple rustic vase to convey the proper wabi-sabi aesthetic. Ideally, the bud would open during the course of the ceremony. In this context, camellia might evoke humility, or simply the quiet beauty of winter. In other quarters, camellia carried a connotation of bad luck. During the days of the samurai, heads literally "fell," much like the camellia *japonica* blossom that falls from the branch, not petal by petal, but all at once: kerplunk! The flower, as if severed, falls to the ground, or into the unfathomable world beyond death, the mysterious "well" of the unknown. In some notable places hundreds of blossoms can be seen scattered en masse on the ground, a beautiful site in itself with its own term, *ochitsubaki*: fallen camellia.

Two days post-election, we didn't yet know whose head would "fall." The suspense and uncertainty increased everyone's already heightened fear and anxiety from COVID to somewhere off the graphs. Mail-in ballots kept pouring in, and day by day states that voted Republican in the last election, the red states; began to turn light blue and then blue: Democrat. This phenomenon, perceived as "fraud," rather than what it really was: a majority of Americans crying out for change; prompted the president to start the rallying cry, "Stop the Steal!" His followers would take it literally.

By the first week of November, 2020, more than camellias and our current head of state would fall. COVID deaths throughout the world reached 1.2 million and counting. Every day the US recorded new milestones of infection. Seven states set records for hospitalizations. Yet not all countries such as ours had lost control of the virus. Some nations had managed to contain COVID-19; some had nearly snuffed it out; but we Americans let it rage on, giving it free will and free rein riding on some kind of twisted definition of liberty. Now the virus seemed unstoppable.

In the first days after the election most of us were preoccupied with last minute ballot counts. There had not been a clear landslide victory for either candidate, and so the country waited for the mystery of the Electoral College to officially award US presidency. COVID news took a back seat for a little while, unless you were one of 68,000 Americans hospitalized with the disease, or you were a friend or family member of one of the 240,000 who had died of COVID, or you were a doctor or nurse who had worked tirelessly for the last 9 months as patient after patient poured into your ICU. For those who had contracted a serious case of COVID, those who staffed the front lines of emergency medical treatment, the pandemic was real, tangible, unlike the flu, and very threatening; it was not a hoax. Doctors continued to plead with the public to follow CDC guidelines, to take it seriously, but their voices seemed to fall on ears closed to anything but conspiracy theories and delusion.

In my little world, protected from the front lines, removed from urban unrest, and relatively free from mass infections, camellias provided a small but pleasant distraction and diversion—and a challenge, as I tried once again to grow one on the mountain, determined to keep it and myself alive and healthy throughout the winter.

In the Time of Chrysanthemum our local nursery had hosted a close out sale. No longer able to hang on to her business with the pandemic restrictions, the owner decided to clear out inventory and try again the following spring. A dozen five-gallon camellias, marked down at ridiculously low prices, proved irresistible. My sister and I bought three—two for her, one for me. Because I'd already failed with C. *hiemalis* and C. *sasanqua*, she took Shishi-Gashira, and Kanjiro. I took the hybrid J.C. Williams, a cross between C. *japonica* and C. *saluenensis*, a rare one, I was told later by a nurseryman, one that was cold hardy, he'd said. This news gave me added confidence in my third attempt to grow a camellia on a windy mountain at 1300 feet. Perhaps I'd finally landed the right one.

Duty bound to protect my prized camellia throughout winter, before our first cold snap, I gave it mulch, plenty of water and a protective "blanket," a white net of polypropylene fabric that lets in sun and rain. I meant to baby my baby as long as it took, to nurture its life force in the face of so much darkness and death.

Care and protection, kindness, knowledge of how life thrives and flourishes: these seemed like noteworthy virtues to cultivate in caring for a camellia, a person or a nation. How would these characteristics unfold as we headed toward the end of 2020 and "perfect vision"? Some had made predictions. Others saw the writing on the wall.

By day four post-election, the Biden-Harris ticket garnered over 270 of the required electoral votes and was, by most reputable sources, declared the winner. But the current president refused to concede and claimed that the Democrats had "stolen" the election, even though not one election monitor or court had found any credible evidence of election fraud; in fact, just the opposite. Most election officials declared 2020 to be one of the most closely monitored and fair elections ever.

Ten days post-election, the president still had not conceded defeat and continued to file lawsuit after lawsuit to either stop the counting of mail-in ballots, to recount existing ones, or dismiss those already counted as fraudulent. Georgia, now a "blue" state, recounted their ballots three times. No massive fraud that would alter the outcome of the election was found in the "peach" state, and not one of the president's lawsuits (50 by mid-December) proved fruitful. In defiance he refused to cooperate in the presidential transition process outlined by the Presidential Transition Act of 1963: "Any disruption occasioned by the transfer of the executive power could produce results detrimental to the safety and well-being of the United States and its people." With our collective anxiety already at a threshold, this new twist of events sent us all, well, off that graph, again. We counted on the federal government to do its duty prescribed under the Constitution, a document we Americans held as nearly "sacred." Then the president fired the Defense Secretary and key senior defense officials. The letter outlining "Ten Things You Need to Know to Stop a Coup," began circulating again. Alarms bells went off as we witnessed the phenomenon of the "big lie," a propaganda technique used to grossly distort facts. The idea is that people are more apt to believe a big lie than a little one, because no one believes that someone could be so audacious. The big lie has been used throughout history by authoritarian regimes (you've all heard their names), and now it seemed someone was trying to mimic one of those "regimes." Even though many Americans had not fallen for the big lie, many more did: a startling 70 million Americans voted for the president's second term, a man who had refused to denounce white supremacy and hate groups, who in fact cultivated them as his base, a man who refused to graciously concede defeat and continued to tell the big lie over and over about a fair election being "stolen."

All the while COVID numbers climbed higher and higher with each day's infectious numbers topping the day before. Our state was no exception, although we were doing better than 45 others. Still Governor Inslee held a special COVID newscast urging Washingtonians to forego Thanksgiving get-togethers, to keep socially distanced, to reduce our "bubbles" of contact, and wear a mask in public at all times.

While the news drama unfurled like a tornado funnel moving ever closer, my sister and I planted the other two camellias at her house and began to make preparations for our Thanksgiving of two. There would be no dinner with siblings and their families, or any walks in the park with friends, or lattes at island coffee shops, or free community dinners for islanders typically organized by churches and non-profits. Instead, we discussed a Zoom meeting but hadn't yet finalized it.

During this time, if I could have been magically transported to Japan, I would have planned a winter outing to view camellias, a delightful respite from anything politically or personally worrisome. Bloom time begins in November and extends into April so the camellia lover had much to choose from over a long period of time. In southern Yamaguchi Prefecture the Wild Camellia Grove of Mt. Kasayama advertised 24 acres with 25,000 camellias and a view of the Sea of Japan in the background. Further south in Nagasaki Prefecture, and boasting the Tamanoura, "one of the rarest camellias in the world," lies the Goto Camellia Forest Park. Going north to the Ito Peninsula, Komuroyama Park beckons with 4000 camellias in 1000 varieties with a view of Mt. Fuji in the background. And in Hyogo, Shiga, Nara and Wakayama prefectures, "little Buddha" camellias: Yabu (Wild Camellia), Kariginu (Hanging Coat), and Karanishiki (Chinese Brocade) among others; would lure pilgrims into the hallowed gardens of Temples No. 6, 14, 18 and 24 (respectively) on the 25 Flower Temple Pilgrimage.

December 1, the ancient Japanese almanac foretold the season: "The North Wind Brushes the Leaves"; and the president still had not conceded defeat. The Camellias Kanjiro and Yuletide began to bloom, and the beauty of bare trees bereft of autumn leaves transported me into that *wabi-sabi* world that appreciates the simple lonely feeling of passing time and transience that the winter season evokes.

On the mountain, a layer of frost decorated the landscape. Vulnerable to the capricious nature of the elements, before heading out on my morning walk, I checked in on J.C. Williams and the condition of his winter blanket. All was well.

That night, secure in my mountain hermitage with food, warmth and a wind protected camellia, I entered a five-day Rohatsu *sesshin* via Zoom to honor Buddha's Enlightenment Day (December 8), and to grapple with whatever emerged from my agitated mind. With COVID cases rising and the president fixated on imaginary election fraud rather than how to stop the virus, I welcomed a week-long retreat and respite from our nation's drama. But with the stakes so high for our country's untested democracy and the downward spiraling health of its citizens, I couldn't stop myself from taking a peek now and then at "breaking news." With new crises and uncertainties erupting every day, I hoped for peace on my cushion, but found it mostly during prescribed work periods when I furiously embarked on washing windows and screens, reorganizing closets and picking up twigs and pine cones from the labyrinth path. Physical activity dispersed anxious energy, softened sharp edges. A dark messy film lifted from house, land and spirit—at least temporarily, until the next glimpse down, that bottomless well.

During the seven days of Rohatsu one million more Americans became infected with the virus, and 10,000 died, one for every minute of every day. The president had yet to concede defeat and continued to play golf, holding intermittent news conferences where he denounced the elections and claimed that Democrats had stolen his second term. His supporters chanted "Stop the Steal!" a rallying cry without any basis in reality, but planted in their minds for all the wrong reasons. The president's lawsuits continued to be thrown out of courts, while Republican governors continued to certify election results from "swing" states without any Republican judge, election official or state's attorney general finding any proof of widespread fraud.

In an article by Andrew Higgins in *The New York Times* titled "The Art of the Lie? The Bigger the Better," the author elaborated on the "big lie" phenomenon, how big lies, used throughout history to manipulate the public, call upon a "tribalist" mentality. One has to go along with the lie whether one believes it or not in order to maintain "membership" in the tribe.

Contemplating the dualistic nature of our world such as the forces of good and evil, right and wrong, lies and truth; the events of 2020 from a bird's eye perspective could be seen as a series of mere tidal movements: conditions under the control of gravitational pull. Our elections, more like a tidal surge with tumultuous waves roiling, and logs the size of tropical trees battering the coast, eventually, for a day or two, rolled into a lull. The tide receded and the ocean calmed. It was temporary. Soon another tide, another storm arose. The cycle continued endlessly, timelessly, patterns of good times and bad times rolling in and rolling out, surging, not surging, composing, calming, the celestial tugs pulling us this way and that like a ride at Water

World, or ocean currents dictated by the force of the moon.

I could see that this American tidal play with its 330 million cast of characters had a role for everyone. The lead role set the other roles in motion, a kind of improvisational drama without any clear direction at times, and other times, a foreshadowing of doom and destruction. This play did not have a director in the usual sense. It was all improv from the beginning, but some caught the gist early on and managed to snag big roles. Those were the actors we saw in the news.

My only role in this play was to vote, to be one of the millions wearing a mask. You could see me in the background, the crowd scenes, walking along the street, going somewhere "essential" with head down and mask on. All the while new characters came onto the stage and others left, like the incoming and outgoing tides, the movement continuous with nothing being permanent or fixed. For awhile I fell into being a detached observer watching the scenes unfold from the sidelines, from the wings. *How interesting! Oh, he played that bit really well. Oh, not so good. She bungled her lines. Hmm! Wouldn't have expected that! Now that's a surprise! Outrageous! No, oh my god... Stop!* Some characters were pretty predictable; others took the improv part to new heights. But this detached observer role, this character in the wings, it too was false, an act, a cover-up for all that festered underneath the surface. On the day of yet another lawsuit (this one to the Supreme Court) intending to overturn our elections, and on the cusp of the tenth federal execution since July (one of a total of 15 the president intended to carry out before the end of his term in January) something putrid and dark began to emerge in my being. It started with a headache and by late afternoon manifested into what felt like a panic attack. Chilly as ice, I started shaking uncontrollably. The thought of a hot bath—the closest thing to being in a comforting womb—soon had me settled into a tub of warm water. The shaking stopped, for awhile. But when I rose from the bath my blood pressure either shot up or plummeted abruptly, and in an unexpected state of spiraling dizziness I collapsed onto the floor. While I lay sprawled out on the cold hardwood wondering what in the world was happening, I thought, maybe I'm going to die. Maybe this is my time. I thought, it might actually be okay, a relief of sorts; then wondered how to get help, how to reach my phone, how to call my sister next door, or 911. My earlier chills moved into sweating, and the cold floor felt soothing on my back. After awhile, maybe 10 or 15 minutes, maybe more, maybe less; I managed to stand up without falling back down. Knowing what was coming next, I grabbed a pail from the bathroom and flopped onto the couch. An hour later the purge began: violent vomiting, every hour, all night long. Food poisoning? Mind and mental poisoning? All the fear and anxiety I'd been holding in my body from the endless crises of 2020 suddenly erupting?

The year had brought a tsunami of upheaval: COVID-19 surging out of control, police killings of unarmed men and women, rioting, demonstrations, fires, smoke, hurricanes, lies, conspiracy theories, millions of Americans living an entirely different reality from mine; and the latest bit of news, the destruction of pristine Sonoran wilderness in the president's last ditch effort to build the Wall; another order to execute one more human life: the only woman on death row. Some residue of all these American tragedies heaved out of my body into a plastic pail in the dark of night.

As I lay in bed waiting for the next wave of putrid vomit to come forth, I could hear the wind blowing through the tall firs. Camellias do not like wind, but my camellia was wrapped in its protective blanket; it had to survive; it must. Both of us were trying to make it through this winter by hanging on to promises of spring warmth and awakening, of reckoning. A vaccine had just been authorized and shipped; the Supreme Court refused to hear the latest lawsuit; the Electoral College certified the election result. But the executions continued, the border wall continued, the denial of losing an election continued. To destroy rather than construct, to take life rather than save it, to lie rather tell the truth, these were the choices being made. And still 70 million Americans chose that, trusted *that*.

Four days after my purge, I spent most of the day in bed unsure how to resume a normal life again. My bedroom window had a ledge where I kept a night lantern, my smart phone and a cold cup of mint tea, the only thing I could stomach. My bed felt like a private bunker, a place one hid for safety in the time of unprecedented disaster. The sun would set and the wind would come up and blow all night; the next morning the sun would rise and the wind would die down. This was the rhythm of my day.

Sometimes I'd wake in the middle of the night and listen to dharma talks on my phone, talks recorded during this year's Rohatsu sesshin, a time when thousands of Zen practitioners throughout the world gathered to sit like Buddha Shakyamuni did when he awakened at the sight of the morning star. Whether Buddhist or not, we were all in our myriad ways trying to touch that star, and the words I remembered were "be kind," "be generous," "pay attention to the present moment and its wonder." Know that in this world of duality we cannot have life without death, health without sickness, peace without war. Sit on your cushion in meditation as an act of faith, a returning over and over to whatever notion you have of True Self. In that moment of coming to the cushion "we declare our allegiance," says Chogyam Trungpa Rinpoche, not to the world of ego folly but the "Great Mystery" that we cannot name.

These dharma talks, recorded at a training monastery, ended with three resonate gongs and an angelic woman's voice chanting the words "four great bodhisattva vows." Her voice, an enchanting sound in the middle of the night, carried into my dreams.

How to live those vows that were so aspirational, so impossible, and yet so vital:

Beings are numberless, I vow to save them.
Delusions are inexhaustible, I vow to end them.
Dharmas are boundless, I vow to enter them.
Buddha's way is unsurpassed, I vow to become it.

On December 30, we broke another COVID record: 3725 deaths in one day; the next day we broke that record with 3900, then 4000, 4100, 4300... The promise of 20 million vaccines by year's end materialized as only 2 million administered—yet another failure of our country to mobilize resources, coordinate efforts, and stop the virus.

In the ancient Japanese calendar, January 1 is not the first day of the new year but only Season #66: "Beneath the Snow the Wheat Sprouts." On January 1, we Americans, still buried like little kernels wanting so badly to become new life, still lived in the realm of 2020; the infamous year persisted. Shodo Harada Roshi, a Rinzai Zen master gave a live stream dharma talk from Japan to his worldwide sanghas. He said, "[N]ow a new year comes, but it is hard to say 'Happy' or 'Great' New Year with millions dying right this minute. It is not a celebrating moment at all..." But he was wrong, there was one very small thing to celebrate: my J.C. Williams began to bloom; it bloomed all that day and night and into January 6, the day of the predicted coup attempt. On that day—the same day that 3915 Americans lost their lives to COVID-19—right-wing insurgents, egged on by the president and his personal attorney, stormed the US Capitol carrying pipes, pistols, zip ties, and Confederate flags. Outside, a makeshift gallows, with noose and steps suggested their intent: "Hang Pence!" the rioters called out. The Vice-President had violated the tribe's code of allegiance; he exercised his constitutional duty rather than circumvent it.

My little pink camellia bloomed all through the insurrection and the five hours that Congress and their staffs hid out from angry mobs behind barricaded doors and under sturdy tables.

The mob banged on doors, broke windows, scaled walls, looted property, and battered police officers. (One officer would later die of his wounds, and one of the insurrectionists would be shot dead by police.) Believing their leader, the president, that the election had been stolen, the outraged mob thought they could stop Congress from certifying the election. They were wrong. Democracy and truth prevailed. Congress convened after the insurgents had been arrested, subdued or driven out. Congress, in some last bit of preserved wisdom, formally accepted—at 4:00 a.m. the following morning—Joe Biden's and Kamala Harris' democratically elected victory as the next president and vice-president of the United States.

As winter wind began its daily assault on the mountain, my camellia held fast. One bloom turned into two, with a row of buds ready to meet the harshness of January's onslaught. My camellia kept on blooming while Democrats impeached the president for the second time—a historic first. It was still blooming on Inauguration Day when 7-foot-high razor fencing and 25,000 National Guard troops surrounded the Capitol to keep our new president and vice-president safe from American terrorists. It continued to bloom the day after, the one-year anniversary of when the first American tested positive in my home state, Washington, and the president said, "We have it totally under control. It's one person coming in from China, and we have it under control. It's going to be just fine." On that day, our one-year anniversary, the US reported over 400,000 deaths from COVID-19.

In the *Shobogenzo*, these words of wisdom, written in the thirteenth century by Zen master and founder of Soto Zen Eihei Dogen, tell us, "It is out of wrong-mindedness and folly that we turn our lives over to the demons of fame and gain, for fame and gain are the great thieves."

My J.C. Williams camellia continued to bloom as I wrote the final words of this story on February 3, the final day of 2020 per the ancient Japanese calendar. The death toll worldwide had surpassed 2.25 million, with the US coming in at 440,000. On February 4, Season #1 proclaimed, "Spring Wind Thaws the Ice," and "a warm wind begins to blow from the east...." It is a time when the first plum blossoms appear, and we celebrate, yet again, another spring, another chance to bloom, to be a Buddha, or simply to find our corner of light.

The following day my sister and I went to a makeshift clinic on the mainland to get our first dose of the COVID-19 vaccine. Bless the nurses! All day long, day after day, week after week, they cheerfully stabbed needles into arms. Sitting there in that chair with the needle going in—painlessly—I didn't know if the tears welling up were those of joy or grief. I had survived. Millions had not.

"Unryu" (Dragon in the Clouds) camellia

Epilogue

We thought the pandemic would end with the arrival of vaccines. We were wrong. For a few short months in 2021 some who were fully vaccinated removed their masks and threw caution to the wind. I remember seeing a maskless neighbor in the grocery store and thinking, nope, keeping mine on for now, thank you—even though I'd received two doses of Pfizer. I knew the virus wasn't done with us. Delta, a more contagious and deadly variant, had already taken off in India; it would soon arrive on our shores. Omicron, yet another variant, even more contagious, would soon follow. Hospitals became overwhelmed—again. Thousands more died. Health care workers were in short supply either because they had left the profession due to burnout and PTSD, were sick with COVID, had died of COVID or had committed suicide because of COVID.

The climate crises continued too. An unprecedented "heat dome" the previous summer, followed by unprecedented flooding in autumn, followed by an unprecedented Arctic storm in winter turned the otherwise mild climate of the Pacific Northwest into a record-breaking statistic on climate charts. Once again, we were in the national news.

At the beginning of 2022, the Year of the Tiger, no one could predict when the pandemic would end. Like the tiger—endangered, stalked, losing her habitat—we stood at the precipice of a timeless white winter, and hesitated. With our democracy still in peril, our climate out of control, our social ills escalating, some had gone down the road of drug addiction and declining mental health with depression and anxiety disorders on the rise. Yet now, and then, and always, nature's beauty, manifesting in leaf or flower, bud or branch, caught our attention and gave us the fortitude to take that next step into the deep drift of future time. We might sink up to our belly in snow, but we took the dare. The sound of raven wings overhead, the sight of a dragonfly, the stark white petals of a Japanese anemone, or the unfathomable depth of a lotus blossom imparted the will to plunge headlong down the mountain of time, our footprints mere shadows in the night.

We, like the tigress, moved slowly, deliberately toward something in the distance. Was it the sound of a song? A bell? An exotic bird? Perhaps it was the scent of plum? Or the color purple?

In the valley, where the snow ends, buds, barely visible, began to emerge from bare branches. Daffodils had begun to push up through black earth. Hellebore, and witch hazel, daphne and camellia, relished the cold and did not turn away, but blossomed in spite of it.

In these times of "unprecedented," we hung on to Joanna Macy's vision of the "Great Turning": a time of transition away from industrial/corporate development, unsustainable living habits, and racial inequality, to a life-sustaining, life-affirming way of being on the planet. We are still, as this book goes to press, in the throes of "Turning," a wild ride on the whims of change and impermanence with an outcome that remains entirely uncertain.

We are the tiger, or tigress. We are time travelers, looking into the unknowable future. We cannot escape our lives, our families, our communities, our nations, or our global interconnectedness. We take a step forward, acknowledge that 5.9 million world citizens have perished from this thing called COVID-19—that 946,000 (and counting) are my fellow countrymen and women—and we carry on. It's a harsh landscape that we move through. It's hard to take the next step at times, but we follow the momentum, the movement, called by something higher, other-worldly, yet of this world because beauty co-exists with the ugly, and joy holds hands with grief, and the whole of it swirls like snowdrifts through our bodies, through our awareness. And then there's a respite, an awakening, the plum tree and daffodil burst into bloom, and we regain our hope and our will to continue.

Plum branches, daffodil and camellia

References

Books

Aitken, Robert. *A Zen Way: Basho's Haiku and Zen*. Second edition: Washington, D.C.: Shoemaker & Hoard. First edition: Weatherhill Inc., 1978.

Beck, Charlotte Joko. *Everyday Zen: Love & Work*. San Francisco: Harper & Row Publishers, 1989.

Blyth, R.H. *Haiku: Volume 1–4*. Tokyo: The Hokuseido Press, 1982.

Dewey, H.E. *Living the Japanese Arts & Ways*. Berkeley: Stone Bridge Press, 2003.

Donegan, Patricia & Ishibashi, Yoshie. *Chiyo-ni: Woman Haiku Master*. Tokyo, Boston, Singapore: Tuttle Publishing, 1998.

Donegan, Patricia. *Haiku Mind: 108 Poems to Cultivate Awareness & Open Your Heart*. Boston & London: Shambhala, 2010.

Finn, Perdita and Strand, Clark. *The Way of the Rose: The Radical Path of the Divine Feminine Hidden in the* Rosary. New York: Penguin Random House, 2019.

Fong, Wen. *Returning Home: Tao-chi's Album of Landscapes and Flowers*. New York: George Braziller, 1976.

Harada, Sekkei. *The Essence of Zen: The Teachings of Sekkei Harada*. Translator: Daigaku Rumme. Boston: Wisdom Publications, 2008.

Hass, Robert. *The Essential Haiku: Versions of Basho, Buson & Issa*. The Ecco Press, 1994.

Lanoue, David G. *Pure Land Haiku: The Art of Priest Issa*. Second Edition: New Orleans: David G. Lanoue, 2016. First Edition: Reno: Buddhist Books International, 2004.

Nakagawa, Soen. (Tanahashi, Kazuaki and Chayat, Roko Sherry translators). *Endless Vow: The Zen Path of Soen Nakagawa*. Boston & London: Shambhala, 1996.

Ryokan, Taigu. Translator: Nobuyuki Yuasa, *The Zen Poems of*

Ryokan. Princeton: University Press, 1981.

Shantideva; Batchelor, Stephen (trans.). A *Guide to Bodhisattva's Way of Life*. Library of Tibetan Works and Archives, 1999.

Shikibu, Murasaki. *The Tale of Genj*. Translator: Edward G. Seidensticker. Penguin Books, 1992.

Shonagon, Sei. *The Pillow Book*. Translator: Meredith McKinney. London: Penguin Books, 2006.

Strand, Clark. *Seeds from a Birch Tree: Writing Haiku and the Spiritual Journey*. New York: Hyperion, 1997.

Walker, Alice. *The Color Purple*. New York: Harcourt Brace Jovanovich, 1982.

Magazines & Newsletters

Atkins, Dr. Paul. "The Enlightenment of Plants and Trees in Noh Drama." Ikebana International Seattle Chapter 19 Newsletter, Issue 7, Summer 2005.

Editorial Staff: *Kado Ikenobo*, October, 2015, (Japanese). "Cosmos." Kyoto: Ikenobo Ikebana Headquarters Publishing.

Endo, Yoshiko. "50 Temples and Their Flowers: A Pilgrimage." *Kateigaho International Edition*, 2010 Spring/Summer edition, Vol. 25, page 96. Tokyo: Sakai Bunka Publishing Inc.

Imperial Head Priest of Daikakuji. "Enjoying the Rain." *Saga Magazine* No. 1040, July, 2018, page 1 (Japanese). Kyoto: Daikakuji Publishing.

McLeod, Melvin and Macy, Joanna. "Joanna Macy on the Great Awakening the Planet Needs." *Lion's Roar*, May 15, 2021. Halifax: Lion's Roar Foundation.

Films

Landry, Christopher. "Joanna Macy and the Great Turning." November 1, 2014. The Video Project.

About the Author

Joan D. Stamm lived in Kobe, Japan in the early '90s where her interest in Zen and ikebana took root. On her return to the States, she continued to practice and study Zen and Tibetan Buddhism for the next thirty years with a variety of notable teachers.

In 2004, a love of nature led Stamm to a remote island in the Salish Sea where she took up residence in 2008. Four years later, she co-founded Cold Mountain Hermitage, a Buddhist study and practice group that moved from in-person to online gatherings during the pandemic. During the second year of the pandemic, Stamm took formal Zen precepts (*Jukai*) with Eido Frances Carney Roshi at the Olympia Zen Center, and was given the Buddhist name Kanka Kyoshin (generous flower, harmonious faith).

A certified teacher in the Saga School of Ikebana, Stamm had been teaching ikebana for 15 years up to the time of the pandemic when she suspended classes to avoid the spread of the virus. During the many months of isolation, she continued to create ikebana and post her photographs online so that others could enjoy this beautiful art form. Stamm hopes to resume teaching in person again some day.

In addition to Stamm's training in meditation, Buddhism and ikebana, she holds an MFA in writing and literature from Bennington College and a BA in art from The Evergreen State College.

For more of Stamm's writing see *A Pilgrimage in Japan: the 33 Temples of Kannon* and *Heaven and Earth are Flowers: Reflections on Ikebana and Buddhism*. To see more of her ikebana and pilgrimage photos please visit her website at: https://joandstamm.com/ or Facebook page at: https://www.facebook.com/joan.d.stamm/.

If you enjoy Stamm's writing, please consider posting a review on your favorite online site, or leave a comment or message for her on Facebook.

MANTRA
BOOKS

EASTERN RELIGION & PHILOSOPHY

We publish books on Eastern religions and philosophies. Books
that aim to inform and explore the various traditions that began in
the East and have migrated West.
If you have enjoyed this book, why not tell other readers by
posting a review on your preferred book site.

Recent bestsellers from MANTRA BOOKS are:

The Way Things Are
A Living Approach to Buddhism
Lama Ole Nydahl
An introduction to the teachings of the Buddha, and how to make use of these teachings in everyday life.
Paperback: 978-1-84694-042-2 ebook: 978-1-78099-845-9

Back to the Truth
5000 Years of Advaita
Dennis Waite
A demystifying guide to Advaita for both those new to, and those familiar with this ancient, non-dualist philosophy from India.
Paperback: 978-1-90504-761-1 ebook: 978-184694-624-0

Shinto: A celebration of Life
Aidan Rankin
Introducing a gentle but powerful spiritual pathway reconnecting humanity with Great Nature and affirming all aspects of life.
Paperback: 978-1-84694-438-3 ebook: 978-1-84694-738-4

In the Light of Meditation
Mike George
A comprehensive introduction to the practice of meditation and the spiritual principles behind it. A 10 lesson meditation programme with CD and internet support.
Paperback: 978-1-90381-661-5

A Path of Joy
Popping into Freedom
Paramananda Ishaya
A simple and joyful path to spiritual enlightenment.
Paperback: 978-1-78279-323-6 ebook: 978-1-78279-322-9

The Less Dust the More Trust

Participating in The Shamatha Project, Meditation and Science
Adeline van Waning, MD PhD
The inside-story of a woman participating in frontline meditation research, exploring the interfaces of mind-practice, science and psychology.
Paperback: 978-1-78099-948-7 ebook: 978-1-78279-657-2

I Know How To Live, I Know How To Die

The Teachings of Dadi Janki: A warm, radical, and life-affirming view of who we are, where we come from, and what time is calling us to do
Neville Hodgkinson
Life and death are explored in the context of frontier science and deep soul awareness.
Paperback: 978-1-78535-013-9 ebook: 978-1-78535-014-6

Living Jainism

An Ethical Science
Aidan Rankin, Kanti V. Mardia
A radical new perspective on science rooted in intuitive awareness and deductive reasoning.
Paperback: 978-1-78099-912-8 ebook: 978-1-78099-911-1

Ordinary Women, Extraordinary Wisdom

The Feminine Face of Awakening
Rita Marie Robinson
A collection of intimate conversations with female spiritual teachers who live like ordinary women, but are engaged with their true natures.
Paperback: 978-1-84694-068-2 ebook: 978-1-78099-908-1

The Way of Nothing
Nothing in the Way
Paramananda Ishaya
A fresh and light-hearted exploration of the amazing reality of
nothingness.
Paperback: 978-1-78279-307-6 ebook: 978-1-78099-840-4

Readers of ebooks can buy or view any of these bestsellers by
clicking on the live link in the title. Most titles are published in
paperback and as an ebook. Paperbacks are available in traditional
bookshops. Both print and ebook formats are available online.

Find more titles and sign up to our readers' newsletter at
http://www.johnhuntpublishing.com/mind-body-spirit.
Follow us on Facebook at https://www.facebook.com/OBooks
and Twitter at https://twitter.com/obooks.